Lingua Latina
Latin – English Interlinear Stories on Roman History

Latin A1 Reader

Brian Smith

Res Gestae Regum Romanorum

Capitulum Primum: Romulus et Remus

Romulus et Remus, gemini fratres, in mundo venerunt. "Ecce, gemini!" obstetrix exclamat.

Romulus and Remus, twin brothers, came into the world. "Look, twins!" the midwife exclaimed.

Amulius, rex Albae Longae et vir malus, fratres in flumen Tiberim misit. "Infantes in flumine relinquentur," inquit.

Amulius, the king of Alba Longa and an evil man, sent the brothers into the Tiber River. "The infants will be left in the river," he said.

Sed miraculum! Lupa, animal silvestre, ad infantium vagitum venit. Lupa eos invenit et, more matris, nutrivit.

But a miracle! A she-wolf, a wild animal, came to the crying of the infants. The wolf found them and, like a mother, nurtured them.

"Mirabile!" pastor Faustulus, qui hoc vidit, dixit.

"Amazing!" said the shepherd Faustulus, who saw this.

Faustulus, pastor bonus, ad lupam accessit et infantes tulit. "Istos educabo," Faustulus uxori suae dicit.

Faustulus, a good shepherd, approached the wolf and took the infants. "I will raise them," Faustulus said to his wife.

Romulus et Remus apud Faustulum creverunt, robusti facti sunt et audaces. "Fratres fortes eritis," Faustulus dixit.

Romulus and Remus grew up with Faustulus, becoming strong and brave. "You will be strong brothers," Faustulus said.

Cum adoleverunt, Romulus et Remus ad Albae Longae redierunt. Numitor, avus eorum, de tyranno Amulio narravit. "Avus noster ab Amulio pulsus est," Remus dixit.

When they grew up, Romulus and Remus returned to Alba Longa. Numitor, their grandfather, told them about the tyrant Amulius. "Our grandfather was driven out by Amulius," Remus said.

Numitor, avus eorum, eorum auxilio, Amulium vicit et interfecit. "Iustitia facta est!" Romulus exclamat.

Numitor, their grandfather, with their help, defeated and killed Amulius. "Justice has been served!" Romulus exclaimed.

Ei Romulus et Remus urbem novam condere statuerunt. "Urbem nostram aedificabimus," Romulus dixit.

Then Romulus and Remus decided to found a new city. "We will build our city," Romulus said.

Fratres ad Palatinum montem venerunt. "Hic urbs nostra erit," Remus dixit.

The brothers came to the Palatine Hill. "Our city will be here," Remus said.

Sed inter fratres de muro urbis certamen ortum est. "Murus altior erit!" Romulus clamat.

But a conflict arose between the brothers over the city wall. "The wall will be higher!" Romulus shouted.

In contentione, Romulus suum fratrem Remum occidit. "Remus cecidit," Romulus lacrimans dixit.

In the struggle, Romulus killed his brother Remus. "Remus has fallen," Romulus said, weeping.

Nunc Romulus solus erat et solus rexit. "Regnabo pro nobis duobus," Romulus dixit.

Now Romulus was alone and ruled alone. "I will reign for both of us," Romulus said.

Romulus urbem "Roma" nominavit, in honorem sui. "Haec Roma erit," Romulus dixit.

Romulus named the city "Rome" in honor of himself. "This will be Rome," Romulus said.

Ita, Roma, urbs aeterna, condita est. "Roma aeterna," populus clamavit.

Thus, Rome, the eternal city, was founded. "Eternal Rome," the people shouted.

Hoc capitulo, historia Romuli et Remi, conditorum urbis Romae, narratur. Ab initio difficili ad conditam urbem, vita fratrum plena dramatis et actionis est.

In this chapter, the story of Romulus and Remus, the founders of the city of Rome, is told. From a difficult beginning to the founding of the city, the brothers' lives were full of drama and action.

Capitulum Secundum: Roma Crescit

Romulus, conditor et rex Romae, magnas res agere incipit. "Populum Romanum aedificabo," Romulus dicit.

Romulus, the founder and king of Rome, begins to do great things. "I will build the Roman people," Romulus says.

Romulus, primus, senatum Romanum constituit. "Senatus consilium urbis erit," in foro Romano dicit.

Romulus, first, established the Roman Senate. "The Senate will be the council of the city," he says in the Roman forum.

Romulus centum viros sapientes eligit ut senatores fiant. "Vos senatores Romae eritis," Romulus viris dicit.

Romulus chose one hundred wise men to become senators. "You will be the senators of Rome," Romulus says to the men.

Roma, urbs parva sed fortis, incipit crescere. "Roma parva nunc est, sed magna erit," Romulus populo promittit.

Rome, a small but strong city, begins to grow. "Rome is small now, but it will be great," Romulus promises the people.

Romulus leges Romanas dat. "Haec leges iustitiae et pacis sunt," Romulus in senatu pronuntiat.

Romulus gives Roman laws. "These are laws of justice and peace," Romulus declares in the Senate.

Vicini, urbis novae potentiam videntes, Romam timent. "Romani fortissimi sunt," vicini inter se dicunt.

The neighbors, seeing the power of the new city, fear Rome. "The Romans are very strong," the neighbors say to each other.

Romulus bellum cum Sabinis oritur. Romulus, dux fortis, Romanos ad bellum ducit. "Pro Roma pugnabimus!" clamat.

War with the Sabines arises. Romulus, a strong leader, leads the Romans into battle. "We will fight for Rome!" he shouts.

Romulus in bello contra Sabinos victoriam reportat. "Victoria nostra est!" Romulus, post proelium, exclamat.

Romulus wins the war against the Sabines. "Victory is ours!" Romulus exclaims after the battle.

Romulus cum vicinis foedera facit. "Pax nobiscum erit," Romulus cum vicinis loquitur.

Romulus makes treaties with the neighbors. "There will be peace with us," Romulus says to the neighbors.

Sub Romulo, Roma magis magisque crescit. "Urbs nostra crescit in magnitudine et potentia," Romulus populo dicit.

Under Romulus, Rome grows more and more. "Our city is growing in size and power," Romulus tells the people.

Romulus primum murum Romae aedificat. "Hoc murus urbem nostram proteget," Romulus operariis imperat.

Romulus builds the first wall of Rome. "This wall will protect our city," Romulus orders the workers.

Romani Romulo, rege suo, fideles manent. "Romulus, rex noster, nos ducit," Romani in foro loquuntur.

The Romans remain loyal to Romulus, their king. "Romulus, our king, leads us," the Romans say in the forum.

Romulus exercitum Romanum instruit. "Exercitus noster fortissimus erit," Romulus militibus dicit.

Romulus builds the Roman army. "Our army will be the strongest," Romulus tells the soldiers.

Roma, sub Romulo, fortis et invicta fiet. "Roma invicta!" cives in viis clamant.

Rome, under Romulus, will become strong and undefeated. "Unconquered Rome!" the citizens shout in the streets.

Romulus, rex magnus, in historia Romana semper manebit. "Romulus, conditor urbis nostrae, semper memorabitur," senex in foro narrat.

Romulus, a great king, will always remain in Roman history. "Romulus, the founder of our city, will always be remembered," an old man says in the forum.

Hoc capitulo, Roma sub Romulo, primo rege suo, a parva urbe ad magnam civitatem crescit. Leges, murus, et exercitus – omnia haec Romulus ad magnitudinem Romae contribuit.

In this chapter, Rome under Romulus, its first king, grows from a small town into a great city. Laws, walls, and the army – all these Romulus contributed to the greatness of Rome.

Capitulum Tertium: Raptae Sabinarum

Romani, urbe nova condita, uxores non habebant. "Uxores nobis necessariae sunt," Romanus in foro dixit.

The Romans, having founded a new city, did not have wives. "Wives are necessary for us," a Roman said in the forum.

Romulus, regi astuto, consilium cepit. "Ludos magnos Romae faciemus," Romulus senatui suadet.

Romulus, a clever king, devised a plan. "We will hold great games in Rome," Romulus advised the Senate.

Ludi Romae magni et splendidi praeparantur. "Spectacula et ludi erunt," Romulus populo nuntiat.

The great and splendid games were prepared in Rome. "There will be shows and games," Romulus announced to the people.

Sabinos, vicinos Romanorum, ad ludos invitavit. "Venite et ludos nostros spectate," Romulus ad Sabinos mittit.

He invited the Sabines, neighbors of the Romans, to the games. "Come and watch our games," Romulus sent word to the Sabines.

In ludo, Romani Sabinas rapuerunt. "Nunc uxores habemus!" Romani inter se clamant.

During the games, the Romans seized the Sabine women. "Now we have wives!" the Romans shouted to each other.

Sabinorum ira contra Romanos magna erat. "Romani nos deceperunt!" Sabinus in concilio dicit.

The anger of the Sabines against the Romans was great. "The Romans have deceived us!" a Sabine said in the council.

Titus Tatius, rex Sabinorum, bellum contra Romanos paravit. "Romae poenas dabunt!" Titus Tatius Sabinis promittit.

Titus Tatius, king of the Sabines, prepared for war against the Romans. "They will pay in Rome!" Titus Tatius promised the Sabines.

Sabinorum exercitus ad Romam venit. "Ad bellum parati sumus," Romulus milites Romanos hortatur.

The army of the Sabines came to Rome. "We are ready for war," Romulus encouraged the Roman soldiers.

Pugna aspera incepta est. "Pro Roma!" Romani clamant. "Pro Sabinis!" Sabinorum clamor respondet.

A fierce battle began. "For Rome!" the Romans shouted. "For the Sabines!" the Sabine cry responded.

In pugna, precibus uxorum Sabinarum pugna cessavit. "Desinite! Nos uxores et matres sumus!" Sabina in medio pugnae clamat.

In the battle, at the pleas of the Sabine women, the fighting ceased. "Stop! We are your wives and mothers!" a Sabine woman shouted in the midst of the battle.

Romani et Sabinique tandem foedus fecerunt. "Pax nobis melior est," Romulus et Titus Tatius concordant.

The Romans and Sabines eventually made a treaty. "Peace is better for us," Romulus and Titus Tatius agreed.

Titus Tatius, post foedus, cum Romulo in Roma regnavit. "Duo reges, una urbs," Romani et Sabinos dicunt.

After the treaty, Titus Tatius ruled in Rome with Romulus. "Two kings, one city," both the Romans and the Sabines said.

Roma, Sabinorum accessione, aucta est. "Roma nunc fortior est," senator Romanus dicit.

Rome, with the addition of the Sabines, grew stronger. "Rome is now stronger," a Roman senator said.

Pax longa inter Romanos Sabinosque fuit. "Pax et amicitia regnant," Romulus in senatu loquitur.

There was a long peace between the Romans and Sabines. "Peace and friendship reign," Romulus said in the Senate.

Hoc capitulo, historia raptae Sabinarum et pugna subsequens inter Romanos et Sabinos narratur. Per dramatis actionesque, pax et unio inter duas gentes illustrantur.

In this chapter, the story of the abduction of the Sabine women and the subsequent battle between the Romans and Sabines is told. Through dramatic actions, peace and unity between the two peoples are illustrated.

Capitulum Quartum: Rex Numa Pompilius

Romulus, primus rex Romae, mortuus est. "Romulus, conditor noster, decessit," Romani in foro lugentes dicunt.

Romulus, the first king of Rome, has died. "Romulus, our founder, has passed away," the Romans say, mourning in the forum.

Numa Pompilius, vir sapiens et pacificus, rex Romanorum factus est. "Pacem et iustitiam sequar," Numa populo promittit.

Numa Pompilius, a wise and peaceful man, was made king of the Romans. "I will pursue peace and justice," Numa promised the people.

Numa, vir pacis, non bellum sed pacem populo Romano dedit. "Bella non quaerimus," Numa in senatu dicit.

Numa, a man of peace, gave the Roman people peace, not war. "We do not seek wars," Numa says in the Senate.

Sacra Romana a Numa instituta sunt. "Deorum voluntatem colamus," Numa sacerdotibus imperat.

Roman sacred rites were established by Numa. "Let us honor the will of the gods," Numa commanded the priests.

Numa templum Vestae, deae focorum, aedificavit. "Hoc templum aeternum erit," Numa dixit cum templum dedicavit.

Numa built the temple of Vesta, the goddess of hearths. "This temple will be eternal," Numa said when he dedicated the temple.

Virgines Vestales, sacerdotes Vestae, a Numa creatae sunt. "Ignis Vestae numquam exstinguetur," Numa Virgini Vestali praecepit.

The Vestal Virgins, priestesses of Vesta, were created by Numa. "The fire of Vesta will never be extinguished," Numa instructed the Vestal Virgin.

Leges religiosas Numa populo dedit. "His legibus deos colamus," Numa populum docebat.

Numa gave religious laws to the people. "By these laws, let us honor the gods," Numa taught the people.

Sub Numa, Roma in pace crevit. "Pax urbi nostrae prosperitatem fert," Numa dixit.

Under Numa, Rome grew in peace. "Peace brings prosperity to our city," Numa said.

Numa iustitiam et aequitatem populo dedit. "Omnibus ius aequum erit," Numa in foro promulgavit.

Numa gave justice and fairness to the people. "There will be equal justice for all," Numa proclaimed in the forum.

Numa calendarium Romanum ordinavit. "Tempora et festa ordinem habebunt," Numa dixit.

Numa organized the Roman calendar. "Times and festivals will have order," Numa said.

Deis Romanis sacra Numa fecit. "Deorum favorem sic meremur," Numa sacerdotibus explicavit.

Numa made sacrifices to the Roman gods. "Thus we earn the favor of the gods," Numa explained to the priests.

Numa populum Romanum docebat, ut mores et leges intelligeret. "Populus noster sapientia crescit," Numa magistris dixit.

Numa taught the Roman people so that they might understand customs and laws. "Our people grow in wisdom," Numa said to the teachers.

Numa sine ullo bello regnavit. "Numa, rex pacificus," populus in viis dicebat.

Numa reigned without any war. "Numa, the peaceful king," the people said in the streets.

In amore populi Romani Numa vixit. "Numa, rex noster, nos amat," matres ad filios suos dixerunt.

Numa lived in the love of the Roman people. "Numa, our king, loves us," mothers said to their sons.

Numa, rex pacificus, in memoria Romana semper manebit. "Numa, rex noster, in historia nostra semper vivet," senex in templo dixit.

Numa, the peaceful king, will remain in Roman memory forever. "Numa, our king, will always live in our history," an old man said in the temple.

Hoc capitulo, regnum Numae Pompilii, secundi regis Romani, et eius pacis amore et legum institutione narratur. Sub Numa, Roma non solum in magnitudine sed etiam in sapientia et iustitia crevit.

In this chapter, the reign of Numa Pompilius, the second king of Rome, and his love of peace and the establishment of laws is told. Under Numa, Rome grew not only in size but also in wisdom and justice.

Capitulum Quintum: Tullus Hostilius

Numa Pompilius, rex pacificus, mortuus est. "Numa, rex noster, decessit," Romani moerentes dicunt.

Numa Pompilius, the peaceful king, has died. "Numa, our king, has passed away," the mourning Romans said.

Tullus Hostilius, vir bellicosus, rex Romanorum factus est. "Bella et victorias sequemur!" Tullus in senatu clamavit.

Tullus Hostilius, a warlike man, became the king of the Romans. "We will pursue wars and victories!" Tullus shouted in the Senate.

Tullus bellum magno studio diligebat. "Maiorem gloriam in bello quaeramus!" Tullus ad populum suum dixit.

Tullus loved war with great enthusiasm. "Let us seek greater glory in battle!" Tullus said to his people.

Bellum inter Romanos et Albos incepit. "Alba Longa nostra erit!" Tullus milites hortatus est.

War began between the Romans and the people of Alba Longa. "Alba Longa will be ours!" Tullus encouraged the soldiers.

Horatii et Curiatii, tres fratres ex utraque parte, pro suis civitatibus pugnaverunt. "Pro Roma pugnamus!" Horatii clamarunt.

The Horatii and Curiatii, three brothers from each side, fought for their cities. "We fight for Rome!" the Horatii shouted.

In aspera pugna, Horatius Romanus solus superstitit. "Pro Roma vici!" Horatius, victor, exclamavit.

In a fierce battle, the Roman Horatius alone survived. "I have won for Rome!" Horatius, the victor, exclaimed.

Tullus, rege audace, victoriam magnam reportavit. "Alba Longa nunc Romae subiecta est," Tullus triumphans nuntiavit.

Tullus, the bold king, won a great victory. "Alba Longa is now subject to Rome," Tullus triumphantly announced.

Sub Tulli regno, Alba Longa Roma subiecta est. "Nunc Roma potentior est," Tullus in foro Romanorum dixit.

Under Tullus' reign, Alba Longa was subjected to Rome. "Now Rome is more powerful," Tullus said in the Roman forum.

Tullus urbis moenia Romae ampliavit. "Urbem nostram muniamus!" Tullus operariis imperavit.

Tullus expanded the walls of the city of Rome. "Let us fortify our city!" Tullus commanded the workers.

Tullus exercitum Romanum magnum habuit. "Exercitus noster invincibilis erit," Tullus ad centuriones suos dixit.

Tullus had a great Roman army. "Our army will be invincible," Tullus said to his centurions.

In bellis, Tullus gloriam magnam quaesivit. "Gloria aeterna nostra erit!" Tullus in concilio militum dixit.

In wars, Tullus sought great glory. "Eternal glory will be ours!" Tullus said in a council of soldiers.

Tullus templum Marti, deo belli, aedificavit. "Marti, deo nostro, hoc templum dedicamus," Tullus in ceremonia dixit.

Tullus built a temple to Mars, the god of war. "To Mars, our god, we dedicate this temple," Tullus said at the ceremony.

Tullus, post multa bella, morbo periit. "Tullus, rex noster, nos reliquit," Romani lugentes narraverunt.

Tullus, after many wars, died of illness. "Tullus, our king, has left us," the mourning Romans said.

Tullus, bellator rex, in historia Romanorum semper manebit. "Tullus, rex fortis et audax," in annalibus Romanorum scriptum est.

Tullus, the warrior king, will always remain in Roman history. "Tullus, the strong and bold king," is written in the annals of the Romans.

Tullus, rex bellator, in memoria populi Romani manet. "Tullus, dux bellicosus, in historia nostra vivet," magister in schola Romanorum dixit.

Tullus, the warrior king, remains in the memory of the Roman people. "Tullus, the warlike leader, will live in our history," a teacher in a Roman school said.

Hoc capitulo, regnum Tulli Hostilii, tertii regis Romani, eiusque amorem belli et expansionem Romae per victorias militares explicatur. Sub Tulli regno, Roma non solum territorium suum ampliavit sed etiam mores bellicosos populi Romani formavit.

In this chapter, the reign of Tullus Hostilius, the third king of Rome, and his love of war and the expansion of Rome through military victories is explained. Under Tullus' reign, Rome not only expanded its territory but also shaped the warlike customs of the Roman people.

Capitulum Sextum: Ancus Marcius

Post mortem Tulli Hostilii, Ancus Marcius, nepos Numae Pompilii, rex Romanorum factus est. "Pacem et iustitiam, sicut avus meus, sequar," Ancus in senatu dixit.

After the death of Tullus Hostilius, Ancus Marcius, grandson of Numa Pompilius, became king of the Romans. "I will pursue peace and justice, like my grandfather," Ancus said in the Senate.

Ancus, rex pacificus, portum Ostiam ad Tiberis ostium aedificavit. "Hic portus commercium nostrum augere potest," Ancus architectis explicavit.

Ancus, a peaceful king, built the port of Ostia at the mouth of the Tiber River. "This port can increase our trade," Ancus explained to the architects.

Pons Sublicius, primus pons Romae, ab Anco instructus est. "Hoc ponte flumen transire possumus," Ancus in inauguratione pontis dixit.

The Sublician Bridge, the first bridge in Rome, was built by Ancus. "With this bridge, we can cross the river," Ancus said at the inauguration of the bridge.

Ancus Latium, regionem vicinam, vicit. "Latium nunc Romae paret," Ancus in triumpho dixit.

Ancus conquered Latium, the neighboring region. "Latium now obeys Rome," Ancus said in his triumph.

Captivos ex Latio Romam adduxit. "Hi captivi nunc cives Romani fient," Ancus populo Romano nuntiavit.

He brought captives from Latium to Rome. "These captives will now become Roman citizens," Ancus announced to the Roman people.

Ancus montem Aventinum, qui extra urbem erat, populo Romano dedit. "In Aventino novi cives habitabunt," Ancus civibus suis dixit.

Ancus gave the Aventine Hill, which was outside the city, to the Roman people. "New citizens will live on the Aventine," Ancus said to his citizens.

Leges novas Ancus dedit. "Leges istae aequitatem in civitate servabunt," Ancus iudicibus et magistratibus suadet.

Ancus gave new laws. "These laws will preserve fairness in the city," Ancus advised the judges and magistrates.

Civitas sub Anci regno magnopere auxit. "Urbs nostra crescet et florebit," Ancus ad senatores suos dixit.

The city greatly increased under Ancus' reign. "Our city will grow and flourish," Ancus said to his senators.

Ancus in populi Romani amore vixit. "Ancus, rex noster, nos amat et protegit," matres ad filios suos in viis dixerunt.

Ancus lived in the love of the Roman people. "Ancus, our king, loves and protects us," mothers said to their sons in the streets.

Ancus rex prudens et iustus erat. "Iustitia nostra in rege nostro est," senex in foro Romano dixit.

Ancus was a wise and just king. "Our justice lies in our king," an old man said in the Roman forum.

Sacra multa Ancus fecit, ut deos Romanos placaret. "Per haec sacra deorum favorem habemus," Ancus sacerdotibus imperavit.

Ancus performed many sacred rites to appease the Roman gods. "Through these rites, we gain the favor of the gods," Ancus commanded the priests.

Sed, infeliciter, Ancus morbo graviter affectus est. "Rex noster aegrotat," rumor per urbem cucurrit.

But, unfortunately, Ancus was severely affected by illness. "Our king is ill," the rumor spread through the city.

Ancus, post regnum prudens et iustum, morbo periit. "Ancus, rex bonus, nos reliquit," Romani lugentes dixerunt.

Ancus, after a wise and just reign, died of illness. "Ancus, the good king, has left us," the mourning Romans said.

Ancus, rex bonus et amatus, in memoria Romanorum manebit. "Ancus, rex qui amavit pacem, semper in cordibus nostris erit," poeta in funere eius dixit.

Ancus, a good and beloved king, will remain in Roman memory. "Ancus, the king who loved peace, will always be in our hearts," a poet said at his funeral.

Ancus Marcius, rex qui Romam in pace et iustitia rexit, semper ut rex bonus in historia Romana memorabitur. "Ancus, rex qui urbem nostram auxit et ornavit, in annalibus nostris vivet," magister in schola dixit.

Ancus Marcius, the king who ruled Rome in peace and justice, will always be remembered as a good king in Roman history. "Ancus, the king who grew and beautified our city, will live in our annals," a teacher said in school.

Hoc capitulo, gesta Anci Marci, quarti regis Romani, eiusque amorem pacis, iustitiae, et expansionis civitatis explicatur. Sub Anci regno, Roma non solum territorium suum ampliavit sed etiam structuras magnas aedificavit et leges iustas dedit.

In this chapter, the deeds of Ancus Marcius, the fourth king of Rome, and his love of peace, justice, and city expansion are explained. Under Ancus' reign, Rome not only expanded its territory but also built great structures and gave just laws.

Capitulum Septimum: Tarquinius Priscus

Post mortem Anci Marci, Tarquinius Priscus, vir Etruscus, rex Romanorum factus est. "Roma sub me florebit," Tarquinius in senatu promittit.

After the death of Ancus Marcius, Tarquinius Priscus, an Etruscan man, became king of the Romans. "Rome will flourish under me," Tarquinius promised in the Senate.

Tarquinius, Etruscorum origine, Romae novas artes et scientias intulit. "Etruscorum sapientiam Romae adferam," Tarquinius amicis suis dixit.

Tarquinius, of Etruscan origin, introduced new arts and sciences to Rome. "I will bring the wisdom of the Etruscans to Rome," Tarquinius said to his friends.

Circus Maximus, magnus locus ludorum, a Tarquinio aedificatus est. "Hic ludi magni et spectacula erunt," Tarquinius populo Romanorum demonstrat.

The Circus Maximus, a great place for games, was built by Tarquinius. "Here there will be great games and spectacles," Tarquinius showed to the Roman people.

Ludi magni a Tarquinio instituti sunt, populo delectationem ferentes. "Ludi isti Romae gloriam augebunt," Tarquinius in inauguratione circi clamat.

Great games were instituted by Tarquinius, bringing joy to the people. "These games will increase Rome's glory," Tarquinius shouted at the inauguration of the circus.

Tarquinius moenia urbis ampliavit, urbem fortificans. "Moenia haec urbem nostram protegent," Tarquinius architectis suis imperavit.

Tarquinius expanded the city's walls, fortifying Rome. "These walls will protect our city," Tarquinius commanded his architects.

Cloacas, systema aquarum subterraneum, Tarquinius fecit. "Cloacae urbis salubritatem conservabunt," Tarquinius urbanis planificatoribus dixit.

Tarquinius built the Cloacae, an underground water system. "These sewers will preserve the city's health," Tarquinius told the city planners.

Bellum cum Sabinis, vicinis Romanorum, ortum est. "Pro Roma et eius gloria pugnabimus!" Tarquinius ad exercitum suum clamat.

War arose with the Sabines, Rome's neighbors. "We will fight for Rome and its glory!" Tarquinius shouted to his army.

Tarquinius in bello contra Sabinos victoriam reportavit. "Per me, Roma victor est!" Tarquinius post proelium triumphans exclamat.

Tarquinius won victory in the war against the Sabines. "Through me, Rome is victorious!" Tarquinius exclaimed triumphantly after the battle.

Tarquinius templum Iovis, regis deorum, in Capitolio aedificavit. "Hoc templum Iovi, patri deorum, dedicamus," Tarquinius in ceremonia dixit.

Tarquinius built the temple of Jupiter, king of the gods, on the Capitoline Hill. "We dedicate this temple to Jupiter, father of the gods," Tarquinius said during the ceremony.

Senatum Romanum auxit, plures senatores addens. "Per hos viros sapientes, Roma bene regetur," Tarquinius senatui suo dicit.

He increased the Roman Senate, adding more senators. "Through these wise men, Rome will be well governed," Tarquinius said to his Senate.

Sub Tarquinio, divitiae et gloria Romae auxerunt. "Roma sub me et divitiis et gloria crescet," Tarquinius mercatoribus et artificibus Romanis promittit.

Under Tarquinius, the wealth and glory of Rome increased. "Rome will grow in both riches and glory under me," Tarquinius promised to Roman merchants and artisans.

Tarquinius, rex magnificus, a filiis Anci, rege priore, insidiis necatus est. "Tarquinius, rex noster, periit," rumor per urbem cucurrit.

Tarquinius, a magnificent king, was killed by the sons of Ancus, the previous king, in a plot. "Tarquinius, our king, has died," the rumor spread through the city.

Tarquinius, rex qui Romam magnifice auxit, semper ut rex magnificus in historia Romae memorabitur. "Tarquinius, rex qui Romam adornavit et auxit," in annalibus scriptum est.

Tarquinius, the king who magnificently enlarged Rome, will always be remembered as a magnificent king in the history of Rome. "Tarquinius, the king who adorned and expanded Rome," is written in the annals.

Tarquinius Priscus, rex Etruscus qui Romam in magnitudinem et gloriam duxit, in memoria populi Romani manebit. "Tarquinius, rex qui Roma in gloriam duxit," poeta in funere eius laudat.

Tarquinius Priscus, the Etruscan king who led Rome to greatness and glory, will remain in the memory of the Roman people. "Tarquinius, the king who led Rome to glory," a poet praised him at his funeral.

Hoc capitulo, regnum Tarquinii Prisci, quinti regis Romani, eiusque aedificationes magnas, victorias, et artes Etruscas Romae introducentes explicatur. Sub Tarquinii regno, Roma non solum moenibus et aedificiis auxit, sed etiam cultura et scientia Etrusca locupletata est.

In this chapter, the reign of Tarquinius Priscus, the fifth king of Rome, and his great buildings, victories, and the introduction of Etruscan arts to Rome are explained. Under Tarquinius' reign, Rome not only grew in walls and buildings, but also was enriched by Etruscan culture and knowledge.

Capitulum Octavum: Servius Tullius

Post mortem Tarquinii Prisci, Servius Tullius, eius gener, rex Romanorum factus est. "Iustitiam et pacem populo dabo," Servius in senatu pollicitus est.

After the death of Tarquinius Priscus, Servius Tullius, his son-in-law, became king of the Romans. "I will give justice and peace to the people," Servius promised in the Senate.

Servius primus census populi fecit, cives Romanos numerans. "Scire debemus quot cives habemus," Servius ad magistratus suos dixit.

Servius was the first to conduct a census of the people, counting Roman citizens. "We must know how many citizens we have," Servius said to his magistrates.

Classium systema, ordo civium secundum divitias, a Servio constitutum est. "Per classes, iura aequa dabimus," Servius explicavit.

The system of classes, an order of citizens according to wealth, was established by Servius. "Through these classes, we will give equal rights," Servius explained.

Moenia urbis Romae ampliavit, urbem fortiori faciens. "Moenia haec urbem nostram protegent," Servius architectis suis imperavit.

He expanded the walls of the city of Rome, making the city stronger. "These walls will protect our city," Servius commanded his architects.

Servius colles urbis, ut Palatinum et Aventinum, munivit. "Colles nostri munimenta sunt," Servius in consilio militari dixit.

Servius fortified the city's hills, such as the Palatine and Aventine. "Our hills are fortifications," Servius said in a military council.

Servius templum Dianae, deae venationis, aedificavit. "Diana, dea nostra, urbi favere debebit," Servius sacerdotibus suis dixit.

Servius built a temple to Diana, the goddess of hunting. "Diana, our goddess, must favor the city," Servius said to his priests.

Iura nova et aequa populo Romano dedit. "Omnibus Romanis iura dabo," Servius in foro promulgavit.

He gave new and equal rights to the Roman people. "I will give rights to all Romans," Servius proclaimed in the forum.

Servius, rex iustus, populum Romanum auxit, civitatem amplians. "Urbs nostra sub me crescet," Servius populo suo dixit.

Servius, a just king, increased the Roman population, expanding the city. "Our city will grow under me," Servius told his people.

Servius in pace et iustitia regnavit, bellum vitans. "Pax et iustitia meliores sunt quam bellum," Servius in senatu loquebatur.

Servius reigned in peace and justice, avoiding war. "Peace and justice are better than war," Servius said in the Senate.

Servius Latium, regionem vicinam, pacavit, sine bello. "Latium nunc pacatum est," Servius nuntiavit.

Servius pacified Latium, the neighboring region, without war. "Latium is now at peace," Servius announced.

Sed, infelix fatum, Servius a filia Tullia et genero Tarquinio Superbo insidiis necatus est. "Servius, rex noster, periit," rumor per urbem cucurrit.

But, in a tragic fate, Servius was killed in a plot by his daughter Tullia and his son-in-law Tarquinius Superbus. "Servius, our king, has died," the rumor spread through the city.

Servius, rex sapiens et bonus, in memoria Romanorum manebit. "Servius, rex qui nos amavit et iura dedit," senex in foro narravit.

Servius, a wise and good king, will remain in the memory of the Romans. "Servius, the king who loved us and gave us laws," an old man told in the forum.

Servius, in amore populi vixit, cives eum valde amaverunt. "Servius, rex noster, semper nos amavit," matres ad filios suos in viis dixerunt.

Servius lived in the love of the people, and the citizens loved him greatly. "Servius, our king, always loved us," mothers said to their sons in the streets.

Servius Tullius, rex qui Romam iuste et sapienter rexit, semper ut rex bonus in historia Romae memorabitur. "Servius, rex qui iustitiam et pacem nobis dedit," in annalibus scriptum est.

Servius Tullius, the king who ruled Rome justly and wisely, will always be remembered as a good king in the history of Rome. "Servius, the king who gave us justice and peace," is written in the annals.

Hoc capitulo, regnum Servii Tullii, sexti regis Romani, eiusque reformae, aedificationes, et pacem, quas urbi attulit, explicatur. Sub Servii regno, Roma non solum in magnitudine et structura crescebat, sed etiam in iustitia et ordine sociali.

In this chapter, the reign of Servius Tullius, the sixth king of Rome, and his reforms, buildings, and the peace he brought to the city are explained. Under Servius' reign, Rome grew not only in size and structure but also in justice and social order.

Ascensio et Gloria Romae

Capitulum Primum: Appropinquatio Gallorum

Galli, gens fortis et ferox, ad Italiam moverunt. "Galli veniunt!"
nuntius Romanis clamavit.

The Gauls, a strong and fierce people, moved towards Italy.
"The Gauls are coming!" a messenger shouted to the Romans.

In Roma, nuntii de Gallis terrorem inter cives sparserunt. "Galli
nos oppugnabunt!" homo in foro exclamavit.

In Rome, news of the Gauls spread terror among the citizens.
"The Gauls will attack us!" a man exclaimed in the forum.

Galli, armis et viribus praestantes, ad flumen Alliam adpropinquaverunt. "Flumen Alliam iam tenemus," Brennus, dux Gallorum, dixit.

The Gauls, superior in arms and strength, approached the River Allia. "We now hold the River Allia," Brennus, the leader of the Gauls, said.

Romani, hostium adventu territi, exercitum paraverunt. "Arma capite, milites Romani!" consul Romanus imperavit.

The Romans, terrified by the arrival of the enemy, prepared their army. "Take up arms, Roman soldiers!" the Roman consul ordered.

Consules Romani, exercitum ad bellum duxerunt. "Pro Roma pugnabimus!" consul alter clamavit.

The Roman consuls led the army to war. "We will fight for Rome!" the other consul shouted.

Galli, magni et fortes, Romanis formidabiles videbantur. "Galli fortiores sunt quam credimus," miles Romanus amico suo susurravit.

The Gauls, large and strong, seemed fearsome to the Romans. "The Gauls are stronger than we thought," a Roman soldier whispered to his friend.

Romani, de futura pugna anxii, arma paraverunt. "Num victoriam habebimus?" iuvenis Romanus timide rogavit.

The Romans, anxious about the upcoming battle, prepared their weapons. "Will we have victory?" a young Roman asked timidly.

Galli in itinere multas terras vastaverunt, villas et agros incendentes. "Galli omnia vastant!" agricola fugiens dixit.

The Gauls ravaged many lands on their way, burning villages and fields. "The Gauls are destroying everything!" a fleeing farmer said.

Brennus, dux Gallorum, provocavit Romanos ad pugnam. "Romani, venite et pugnate!" Brennus magna voce clamavit.

Brennus, the leader of the Gauls, challenged the Romans to battle. "Romans, come and fight!" Brennus shouted loudly.

Romani, Brenni provocatione accepta, ad Alliam flumen processerunt. "Ad Alliam procedimus!" centurio militibus suis imperavit.

The Romans, having accepted Brennus's challenge, marched to the River Allia. "We march to the Allia!" the centurion ordered his soldiers.

Galli, bello parati, ad Alliam flumen steterunt. "Hodie pugnabimus!" Brennus suis militibus dixit.

The Gauls, ready for battle, stood at the River Allia. "Today we will fight!" Brennus said to his soldiers.

Romani strategiam belli constituerunt, aciem instruentes. "Ordinem servate!" tribunus militum clamavit.

The Romans devised a battle strategy, arranging their battle lines. "Keep your formation!" the military tribune shouted.

Galli, pugnae cupidi, clamorem terribilem fecerunt. "Galli nos terrent," miles Romanus tremens dixit.

The Gauls, eager for battle, let out a terrible shout. "The Gauls terrify us," a trembling Roman soldier said.

Dies pugnae advenit, sol in caelo ardens. "Hodie pro Roma pugnabimus," consul Romanus militibus suis dixit.

The day of battle arrived, the sun blazing in the sky. "Today we will fight for Rome," the Roman consul told his soldiers.

In hoc capitulo, appropinquatio Gallorum ad Romanum imperium et timor ac praeparatio Romanorum ad imminentem pugnam contra Gallos describitur. Galli, fortes et terribiles, minantur Romanis, qui anxi sunt de futuro suo et patriae.

In this chapter, the approach of the Gauls to the Roman Empire and the fear and preparation of the Romans for the imminent battle against the Gauls is described. The Gauls, strong and terrifying, threaten the Romans, who are anxious about their future and that of their homeland.

Capitulum Secundum: Pugna ad Alliam

Pugna ad Alliam flumen terribilis coepit. "Ad pugnam!" dux Romanus clamavit.

The terrible battle at the River Allia began. "To battle!" the Roman leader shouted.

Galli impetum fortem et ferocem fecerunt. "In hostes!" Brennus, dux Gallorum, suis militibus imperavit.

The Gauls made a strong and fierce charge. "Against the enemy!" Brennus, the leader of the Gauls, ordered his soldiers.

Romani, quamquam fortes, resistere conati sunt. "State firmi!" consul Romanus militibus suis hortatus est.

The Romans, though brave, tried to resist. "Stand firm!" the Roman consul urged his soldiers.

Vis Gallorum ingens et formidabilis erat. "Galli valde fortes sunt!" Romanus in acie clamavit.

The strength of the Gauls was immense and terrifying. "The Gauls are very strong!" a Roman shouted in the battle line.

Romani, Gallorum impetu oppressi, a campo pugnae cedere coeperunt. "Nos superant!" miles Romanus timide dixit.

The Romans, overwhelmed by the Gauls' charge, began to retreat from the battlefield. "They are defeating us!" a Roman soldier said timidly.

Consules Romani milites adhortabantur, sed frustra. "Nolite cedere!" alter consul exclamavit.

The Roman consuls encouraged the soldiers, but in vain. "Do not retreat!" the other consul exclaimed.

Galli, stratagema bellum utentes, Romanos circumvenerunt. "Circumvenimus eos!" Gallus clamavit.

The Gauls, using a war strategy, surrounded the Romans. "We have surrounded them!" a Gaul shouted.

Pugna valde aspera erat, et multi cadebant. "Pro Roma!" Romanus moriens susurravit.

The battle was very harsh, and many were falling. "For Rome!" a dying Roman whispered.

Romani multos milites amiserunt, campo sanguine madente. "Fratres nostri ceciderunt," Romanus fugiens dixit.

The Romans lost many soldiers, with the field soaked in blood. "Our brothers have fallen," a fleeing Roman said.

Galli, Romanorum fugam videntes, magis incitati sunt. "Fugiunt!" Brennus risit.

The Gauls, seeing the Romans flee, became even more eager. "They are running away!" Brennus laughed.

Brennus, victoriam iam in manibus sentiens, laetus erat. "Victoria nostra est!" exclamavit.

Brennus, already feeling victory in his grasp, was overjoyed. "Victory is ours!" he exclaimed.

Romani, clade superati, ad urbem Romam fugerunt. "Ad urbem! Salvi esse debemus!" Romanus ex acie clamavit.

The Romans, defeated in disaster, fled to the city of Rome. "To the city! We must be safe!" a Roman shouted from the battlefield.

Galli, victores, spolia et praeda cepere, acie relicta. "Haec omnia nostra sunt," Gallus inter spolia inquit.

The victorious Gauls took spoils and loot, leaving the battlefield behind. "All of this is ours," a Gaul said among the spoils.

Romani de eventu desperati, urbe adhuc minata, trepidabant. "Quid nunc faciemus?" senator Romanus timide rogavit.

The Romans, despairing over the outcome and with the city still threatened, were trembling. "What shall we do now?" a Roman senator asked timidly.

Dies Alliensis clades magna Romana fuit, memoria doloris plena. "Alliensis dies infaustus nobis fuit," Romanus in urbe susurravit.

The day of Allia was a great disaster for the Romans, full of painful memories. "The day of Allia was unlucky for us," a Roman whispered in the city.

Hoc capitulo, pugna ad Alliam flumen et clades quae Romanis accidit, cum terrore et desperatione post pugnam describitur. Galli, fortes et invicti, Romanos superaverunt, et clades Alliensis diu in memoria populi Romani mansit.

In this chapter, the battle at the River Allia and the disaster that befell the Romans are described, along with the terror and despair after the battle. The Gauls, strong and undefeated, overcame the Romans, and the disaster of Allia remained long in the memory of the Roman people.

Capitulum Tertium: Roma in Periculo

Nuntii, pavidi et anhelantes, cladem Romanorum ad Romam portaverunt. "Galli vicimus!" nuntius in foro clamavit.

Messengers, frightened and breathless, brought news of the Roman defeat to Rome. "The Gauls have defeated us!" the messenger shouted in the forum.

Romani, auditis nuntiis, terrore affecti sunt. "Galli adveniunt!" mulier in via exclamavit.

The Romans, hearing the news, were struck with terror. "The Gauls are coming!" a woman exclaimed in the street.

Senatus Romanus cito convocatus est de defensione urbis cogitare. "Urbem defendere debemus!" senator dixit.

The Roman Senate was quickly convened to think about the defense of the city. "We must defend the city!" a senator said.

Muros urbis Romae celeriter firmaverunt. "Muros fortiores facite!" praefectus operariorum imperavit.

They quickly reinforced the walls of the city of Rome. "Make the walls stronger!" the overseer of the workers commanded.

Mulieres et liberi ad loca tuta missi sunt, timore pleni. "Salvi esse debemus," mater filium suum tenens dixit.

Women and children were sent to safe places, full of fear. "We must be safe," a mother said, holding her son.

Galli, armis et clamoribus terribilibus, ad portas Romae appropinquaverunt. "Ecce, Galli!" vigiliae in muris clamaverunt.

The Gauls, with terrible weapons and cries, approached the gates of Rome. "Look, the Gauls!" the guards on the walls shouted.

Romani, fortes sed trepidi, portas urbis fortiter custodierunt. "Portas custodi!" centurio militibus suis clamavit.

The Romans, brave but anxious, guarded the city gates firmly. "Guard the gates!" the centurion shouted to his soldiers.

Galli, magnis copiis, urbem obsidere coeperunt. "Romam capiemus!" Brennus, dux Gallorum, suis militibus dixit.

The Gauls, with great forces, began to besiege the city. "We will take Rome!" Brennus, the leader of the Gauls, said to his soldiers.

In urbe, inopia ciborum et aquae crevit. "Fames nos premit," civis Romanus in via susurravit.

In the city, the scarcity of food and water grew. "Hunger is pressing on us," a Roman citizen whispered in the street.

Quidam Romani de deditione cogitaverunt, desperati. "Forsitan dedere debemus," senator quidam alii suggerit.

Some Romans, desperate, thought about surrendering. "Perhaps we should surrender," one senator suggested to another.

Galli, fortiter et audacter, moenia urbis temptare coeperunt. "Muros eorum frangemus!" Gallus ad alium dixit.

The Gauls, boldly and fearlessly, began to attack the city's walls. "We will break their walls!" one Gaul said to another.

Romani, licet exhausti, resistere pergebant, fortitudinem ostendentes. "Non cedemus!" miles Romanus in muris exclamavit.

The Romans, though exhausted, continued to resist, showing their strength. "We will not yield!" a Roman soldier exclaimed from the walls.

Galli varias machinationes adhibuerunt, ut urbem caperent. "Machinas ad murum move!" Brennus imperavit.

The Gauls used various siege engines to capture the city. "Move the machines to the wall!" Brennus commanded.

Romani in Capitolio, loco tutissimo, fortitudinem et spem servaverunt. "In Capitolio salvi erimus," pater ad filiam suam dixit.

The Romans on the Capitoline Hill, the safest place, maintained their strength and hope. "We will be safe on the Capitoline," a father said to his daughter.

Obsidio longa et dura erat, dies et noctes sine requie. "Quam diu hoc durabit?" civis Romanus, vultu fatigato, amico suo rogavit.

The siege was long and harsh, lasting days and nights without rest. "How long will this last?" a Roman citizen, with a tired face, asked his friend.

In hoc capitulo, descriptio est Romae obsidionis a Gallis et modi quibus Romani urbem suam defenderunt. Timor, desperatio, et fortitudo Romanorum in hac gravi hora illustrantur, cum Galli urbem obsident et Romani in summa desperatione resistunt.

In this chapter, the siege of Rome by the Gauls is described and the ways in which the Romans defended their city. The fear, despair, and strength of the Romans in this grave hour are illustrated as the Gauls besiege the city and the Romans resist in the utmost desperation.

Capitulum Quartum: Capitolium Obsessum

Capitolium, ultima arx Romae, a Gallis obsessa est. "Capitolium tenemus!" Gallus ad alios clamavit.

The Capitoline, the last stronghold of Rome, was besieged by the Gauls. "We hold the Capitoline!" a Gaul shouted to the others.

Galli, fortiter et callide, ad Capitolium ascendere temptaverunt. "Muros scalabimus!" Brennus, dux Gallorum, suis militibus imperavit.

The Gauls, bravely and cleverly, attempted to climb to the Capitoline. "We will scale the walls!" Brennus, the leader of the Gauls, commanded his soldiers.

Romani in Capitolio, quamquam siti et fame laborantes, fortes erant. "Hic stamus!" centurio Romanus militibus suis dixit.

The Romans on the Capitoline, though suffering from thirst and hunger, remained strong. "Here we stand!" a Roman centurion told his soldiers.

Cotidie Galli Capitolium oppugnabant, machinis et viribus. "Capitolium capiemus!" Gallus exultans clamavit.

Every day, the Gauls attacked the Capitoline with machines and force. "We will take the Capitoline!" an exultant Gaul shouted.

Romani intra Capitolium fame laborabant, cibum aquamque desiderantes. "Fames nos urget," civis Romanus tristis dixit.

The Romans within the Capitoline were suffering from hunger, craving food and water. "Hunger is pressing us," a sad Roman citizen said.

Galli murum Capitolii subruere conati sunt, sed frustra. "Hunc murum frangere non possumus!" Gallus frustratus exclamavit.

The Gauls tried to undermine the Capitoline wall, but in vain. "We cannot break this wall!" a frustrated Gaul exclaimed.

Romani, semper vigilantes, in vigiliis nocturnis erant, metu pleni. "Vigilate!" Romanus ad custodes dixit.

The Romans, always watchful, were on night watches, full of fear. "Stay alert!" a Roman told the guards.

Anseres in Capitolio, sacri Iunoni, vigilias servabant. "Anseres nos monent," sacerdos Romanus ad populum dixit.

The geese on the Capitoline, sacred to Juno, kept watch. "The geese are warning us," a Roman priest said to the people.

Nocte quadam, Gallorum furtiva ascensio per ansere detecta est. "Galli ascendunt!" vigilia exclamavit.

One night, the stealthy ascent of the Gauls was detected by the geese. "The Gauls are climbing!" a watchman exclaimed.

Romani, impetu Gallorum detecto, eos fortiter repulerunt. "Repellite hostes!" miles Romanus clamavit.

The Romans, having detected the Gauls' attack, repelled them with great strength. "Repel the enemies!" a Roman soldier shouted.

Obsidio Capitolii longa et dura erat, sine fine visa. "Quam diu hoc sustinebimus?" Romanus anxius rogavit.

The siege of the Capitoline was long and harsh, seeming endless. "How long can we endure this?" an anxious Roman asked.

Romani in auxilium deorum sperabant, preces et sacrificia offerentes. "Dei, adiuvate nos," sacerdos in templo oravit.

The Romans hoped for the help of the gods, offering prayers and sacrifices. "Gods, help us," a priest prayed in the temple.

Galli, victoriam desiderantes, non destiterunt Capitolium oppugnare. "Capitolium nostrum erit," Gallus ambitiosus dixit.

The Gauls, desiring victory, did not stop attacking the Capitoline. "The Capitoline will be ours," an ambitious Gaul said.

Et Romani et Galli proelio fessi erant, sed nullus cedere volebat. "Lassus sum, sed pugnabo," Romanus fatigatus inquit.

Both the Romans and the Gauls were weary from battle, but no one wanted to surrender. "I am tired, but I will fight," a weary Roman said.

Pax inter Romanos et Gallos quaerebatur, ut finis obsidioni fieret. "Pacem faciamus," senator Romanus aliis senatoribus suadebat.

Peace between the Romans and Gauls was sought to end the siege. "Let us make peace," a Roman senator urged the other senators.

Hoc capitulo, drama obsidionis Capitolii a Gallis et resistentia fortis Romanorum in arce ultima urbis describitur. Fames, desperatio, vigilantes ansere et conatus Gallorum urbem capere, omnia ad intensum et dramaticum narrativum contribuunt.

In this chapter, the drama of the Gauls' siege of the Capitoline and the strong resistance of the Romans in the city's last stronghold is described. Hunger, desperation, the watchful geese, and the Gauls' efforts to capture the city all contribute to an intense and dramatic narrative.

Capitulum Quintum: Pactum Cum Gallis

Romani, obsidione defessi, de pace cum Gallis tractare coeperunt. "Pacem petere debemus," senator Romanus in senatu dixit.

The Romans, weary from the siege, began to negotiate peace with the Gauls. "We must seek peace," a Roman senator said in the Senate.

Brennus, dux Gallorum, pacem duram proposuit. "Aurum magnum nobis date," Brennus Romanis imperavit.

Brennus, the leader of the Gauls, proposed harsh terms of peace. "Give us a great amount of gold," Brennus demanded of the Romans.

Romani, libertatem cupientes, aureum pondus pro pace promiserunt. "Aurum dabimus," consul Romanus, tristis, respondit.

The Romans, desiring their freedom, promised a weight of gold in exchange for peace. "We will give the gold," the Roman consul replied sadly.

Galli, dolo usi, pondera falsa in stateram posuerunt. "Galli nos fallunt!" Romanus, observans, susurravit.

The Gauls, using deception, placed false weights on the scale. "The Gauls are cheating us!" a Roman observer whispered.

Brennus, stateram falsam inspectans, "Vae victis!" exclamavit, iniquitate gaudens. "Infelices sumus," Romanus, aurum portans, gemebat.

Brennus, inspecting the false scale, exclaimed, "Woe to the vanquished!" rejoicing in the injustice. "We are unfortunate," a Roman carrying the gold groaned.

Romani, pacis necessitate coacti, conditiones acceperunt. "Pacem accipimus," consul Romanus Brenno dixit.

The Romans, forced by necessity for peace, accepted the terms. "We accept peace," the Roman consul said to Brennus.

Aurum magnum Gallis datum est, pacem ementes. "Hoc aurum pro libertate nostra est," Romanus, aurum tradens, dixit.

A great amount of gold was given to the Gauls, buying peace. "This gold is for our freedom," a Roman said, handing over the gold.

Galli, auro accepto, tandem ab urbe discesserunt. "Galli abeunt!" puer in via clamat.

The Gauls, having accepted the gold, finally departed from the city. "The Gauls are leaving!" a boy shouted in the street.

Romani, Gallis discedentibus, libertatem suam recuperaverunt. "Libertas nostra restituta est!" Romanus in Capitolio laetatus est.

The Romans, with the Gauls departing, regained their freedom. "Our freedom is restored!" a Roman rejoiced on the Capitoline.

Urbs Romae vastata et destructa erat, desolatione plena. "Urbs nostra in ruinis est," mulier in viis lamentans inquit.

The city of Rome was devastated and destroyed, full of desolation. "Our city is in ruins," a woman lamented in the streets.

Romani, urbe vastata, urbem restaurare coeperunt. "Romam aedificemus," architectus Romanus operariis imperavit.

The Romans, with the city devastated, began to rebuild. "Let us build Rome again," a Roman architect ordered the workers.

Senatus Romanus populum ad laborem et reconstructionem hortatus est. "Omnes ad opus!" senator populo imperavit.

The Roman Senate urged the people to labor and rebuild. "Everyone to work!" a senator commanded the people.

Romani, nova spe et virtute, urbem suam renovare coeperunt. "Roma iterum florebit," pater ad filium suum dixit.

The Romans, with new hope and strength, began to renew their city. "Rome will flourish again," a father said to his son.

Roma, cum tempore et labore, paulatim reficiebatur. "Videte, Roma resurgit!" civis Romanus amico suo demonstravit.

Rome, with time and effort, was gradually being restored. "Look, Rome is rising again!" a Roman citizen pointed out to his friend.

Romani, inter ruinas urbis, de futura gloria Romae cogitaverunt. "Roma maior erit," senex, stellas spectans, cogitavit.

The Romans, among the ruins of the city, thought about the future glory of Rome. "Rome will be greater," an old man thought, gazing at the stars.

Hoc capitulo, pactum pacis inter Romanos et Gallos, quod finem obsidioni posuit, et subsequens reconstructio urbis Romae post vastationem Gallicam describitur. Romani, libertatem recuperantes, spem in futurum et determinationem in reaedificatione urbis demonstrant.

In this chapter, the peace agreement between the Romans and Gauls, which ended the siege, and the subsequent rebuilding of the city of Rome after the Gallic devastation are described. The Romans, regaining their freedom, demonstrate hope for the future and determination in rebuilding the city.

Capitulum Sextum: Ancus Marcius

Post mortem Tulli Hostilii, Ancus Marcius, vir pacis et iustitiae, rex Romanorum factus est. "Pacem et iustitiam sequar," Ancus in senatu dixit.

After the death of Tullus Hostilius, Ancus Marcius, a man of peace and justice, became king of the Romans. "I will follow peace and justice," Ancus said in the Senate.

Ancus, portum Ostiam ad mare aedificavit, navigatio et commercium augens. "Portus Ostia magnam utilitatem urbi adferet," Ancus architectis suis explicavit.

Ancus built the port of Ostia by the sea, increasing navigation and trade. "The port of Ostia will bring great benefit to the city," Ancus explained to his architects.

Pontem Sublicium super Tiberim fecit, urbi et regionibus coniungendis. "Hoc ponte urbs et regio coniungentur," Ancus operariis imperavit.

He built the Sublician Bridge over the Tiber to connect the city with the surrounding regions. "With this bridge, the city and region will be connected," Ancus ordered the workers.

Ancus Marcius bellum in Latium gessit et victoriam reportavit. "Latium nunc Romae paret," Ancus post victoriam nuntiavit.

Ancus Marcius waged war in Latium and achieved victory. "Latium now obeys Rome," Ancus announced after the victory.

Multos captivos ex Latio Romam adduxit, eos in civitatem integrans. "Hi captivi nunc Romani erunt," Ancus ad senatum dixit.

He brought many captives from Latium to Rome, integrating them into the city. "These captives will now be Romans," Ancus said to the Senate.

Ancus montem Aventinum, extra muros urbis situm, populo dedit. "In Aventino novi cives habitabunt," Ancus in concione populi dixit.

Ancus gave the Aventine Hill, located outside the city walls, to the people. "New citizens will live on the Aventine," Ancus said in an assembly of the people.

Leges novas et aequas Ancus dedit, iustitiam in civitate firmandam. "Leges istae aequitatem servabunt," Ancus in foro promulgavit.

Ancus gave new and fair laws to establish justice in the city. "These laws will preserve equality," Ancus proclaimed in the forum.

Sub Anci regno, civitas Romana auxit et floruit. "Urbs nostra crescit," Ancus, urbis progressum inspectans, laetus inquit.

Under the reign of Ancus, the Roman city grew and flourished. "Our city is growing," Ancus said happily, observing the city's progress.

Ancus Marcius in populi Romani amore vixit, populum benigne regens. "Ancus, rex noster, nos amat," Romanus in via ad amicum suum dixit.

Ancus Marcius lived in the love of the Roman people, ruling them kindly. "Ancus, our king, loves us," a Roman said to his friend in the street.

Ancus, rex prudens et iustus, semper ad civitatis bonum laboravit. "Rex noster sapientiam et iustitiam amat," senex in foro loquebatur.

Ancus, a wise and just king, always worked for the good of the city. "Our king loves wisdom and justice," an old man was saying in the forum.

Sacra multa Ancus fecit, deorum Romanorum favorem quaerens. "Per haec sacra deos placabimus," Ancus sacerdotibus suis mandavit.

Ancus performed many sacred rites, seeking the favor of the Roman gods. "Through these rites, we will appease the gods," Ancus instructed his priests.

Infeliciter, Ancus morbo gravissimo periit, omnes Romani lugentes. "Ancus, rex bonus, nos reliquit," civis Romanus in foro cum lacrimis dixit.

Unfortunately, Ancus died from a grave illness, and all the Romans mourned. "Ancus, the good king, has left us," a Roman citizen said tearfully in the forum.

Ancus Marcius, rex bonus et amatus, in memoria Romanorum semper manebit. "Ancus, rex qui pacem et iustitiam amavit, semper in cordibus nostris erit," poeta in funere eius laudavit.

Ancus Marcius, a good and beloved king, will always remain in the memory of the Romans. "Ancus, the king who loved peace and justice, will always be in our hearts," a poet praised him at his funeral.

Hoc capitulo, regnum Anci Marci, quarti regis Romani, eiusque amorem pacis, iustitiae, et expansionis civitatis explicatur. Sub Anci regno, Roma non solum territorium suum ampliavit sed etiam structuras magnas aedificavit et leges iustas dedit.

In this chapter, the reign of Ancus Marcius, the fourth king of Rome, and his love for peace, justice, and the expansion of the city is explained. Under Ancus' reign, Rome not only expanded its territory but also built great structures and gave just laws.

Capitulum Septimum: Restitutio Fortitudinis

Romani, clade Gallica superati, se restituerunt. "Romam reficiemus!" consul in senatu dixit.

The Romans, having been defeated by the Gauls, restored themselves. "We will rebuild Rome!" the consul said in the Senate.

Exercitus Romanus reformatus et roboratus est. "Milites fortiores nunc habemus," dux Romanus ad legiones suas dixit.

The Roman army was reformed and strengthened. "We now have stronger soldiers," the Roman general said to his legions.

Disciplina militaris in exercitu renovata est. "Arte militari meliore utemur," centurio ad milites suos inquit.

Military discipline in the army was renewed. "We will use better military tactics," the centurion said to his soldiers.

Novi duces et imperatores electi sunt, rei militaris periti. "Ducem novum eligemus," senator in concilio dixit.

New leaders and commanders, experienced in military matters, were elected. "We will elect a new leader," a senator said in the council.

Romani vicinas gentes in proeliis superaverunt. "Vicimus!" miles Romanus in pugna clamavit.

The Romans defeated neighboring peoples in battles. "We have won!" a Roman soldier shouted in the fight.

Potentia Romae in Italia coepit augeri. "Italia sub Roma erit," consul optimiste praedixit.

The power of Rome began to grow in Italy. "Italy will be under Rome," the consul predicted optimistically.

Foedera cum vicinis civitatibus facta sunt, pacem et stabilitatem augentes. "Pacem cum vicinis faciemus," legatus Romanus dixit.

Treaties were made with neighboring cities, increasing peace and stability. "We will make peace with our neighbors," a Roman envoy said.

Roma in Italia principatum tenebat, omnibus notum. "Roma caput Italiae est," civis in foro loquebatur.

Rome held leadership in Italy, known to all. "Rome is the capital of Italy," a citizen was saying in the forum.

Arte bellica Romani excellebant, victorias celebrantes. "In arte militari nemo nobis par est," miles glorians inquit.

The Romans excelled in the art of war, celebrating victories. "No one is equal to us in military skill," a soldier said proudly.

Legiones Romanae invictae fiebant, innumeris victoriis. "Legio nostra invicta est," legatus legionis dixit.

The Roman legions became undefeated, with countless victories. "Our legion is undefeated," the legion commander said.

Roma exemplar virtutis et potentiae in mundo facta est. "Exemplum sumus omnibus," senator Romanus ad populum dixit.

Rome became an example of virtue and power in the world. "We are an example to all," a Roman senator said to the people.

Nomen Romanum in terris notum fiebat, fama eius longe perveniens. "Nomen Romanum per terras resonat," mercator Romanus dixit.

The Roman name became known in lands far and wide, its fame spreading. "The Roman name echoes throughout the lands," a Roman merchant said.

Roma a civitate parva ad imperium magnum crescebat. "Imperium nostrum augemus," praetor urbanus inquit.

Rome grew from a small city to a great empire. "We are expanding our empire," the urban praetor said.

Romani gloriam et honorem per orbem terrarum quaerebant. "Gloriam et honorem Romae augebimus," generalis Romanus dixit.

The Romans sought glory and honor throughout the world. "We will increase the glory and honor of Rome," a Roman general said.

Historia Romana novam paginam vertit, a clade ad gloriam. "Nova pagina historiae nostrae incipit," magister in schola Romana discipulis suis narravit.

Roman history turned a new page, from defeat to glory. "A new page of our history begins," a teacher told his students in a Roman school.

Hoc capitulo, restitutio et fortitudo Romanorum post cladem Gallicam describitur. Reformatio exercitus, augmentatio potentiae in Italia, et quaestio gloriae et honoris sub novis ducibus et imperatoribus illustrantur. Roma, post difficultates, ad novam gloriam et potentiam ascendit.

In this chapter, the restoration and strength of the Romans after the Gallic defeat is described. The reform of the army, the increase of power in Italy, and the pursuit of glory and honor under new leaders and commanders are illustrated. Rome, after its hardships, rose to new glory and power.

Capitulum Octavum: Gloria Romae Renovata

Post vastationem Gallicam, Roma nova virtute et splendore fulgebat. "Roma nunc fortior est," consul in foro dixit.

After the Gallic devastation, Rome shone with new strength and splendor. "Rome is now stronger," the consul said in the forum.

Civitas in omnes artes et scientias mirum in modum crevit. "In scientiis et artibus excellebimus," magister in schola Romana discipulis suis dixit.

The city grew remarkably in all the arts and sciences. "We will excel in the sciences and arts," a teacher told his students in a Roman school.

Roma, potentia et cultura, caput mundi facta est. "Nunc Roma caput mundi est," senator Romanus in senatu declaravit.

Rome, in power and culture, became the capital of the world. "Now Rome is the capital of the world," a Roman senator declared in the Senate.

Cultura et ars Romanae in urbe floruerunt, talentis et ingenio. "Ars Romana omnibus nota est," artifex in officina sua dixit.

Roman culture and art flourished in the city, through talents and ingenuity. "Roman art is known to all," an artist said in his workshop.

Romani in litteris et philosophia praestantes erant. "Litteris et philosophiae studeamus," philosophus in academia Romana dixit.

The Romans excelled in literature and philosophy. "Let us study literature and philosophy," a philosopher said in a Roman academy.

Leges Romanae ubique in orbe terrarum laudatae sunt. "Leges nostrae exemplar iustitiae sunt," iurisconsultus Romanus in curia dixit.

Roman laws were praised everywhere in the world. "Our laws are an example of justice," a Roman jurist said in the courthouse.

Exemplum Romae a multis aliis civitatibus imitabatur. "Omnes Romam imitantur," peregrinus ad amicum suum in foro Romano dixit.

The example of Rome was imitated by many other cities. "Everyone imitates Rome," a foreigner said to his friend in the Roman forum.

Pax Romana, imperii virtute, in provinciis regnabat. "Pax Romana nobis securitatem dat," civis in provincia Romana dixit.

The Pax Romana, by the power of the empire, reigned in the provinces. "The Roman peace gives us security," a citizen in a Roman province said.

Roma magnificis aedificiis et monumentis exstruebatur. "Videte, quam pulchra est Roma!" puer in via exclamavit.

Rome was built up with magnificent buildings and monuments. "Look, how beautiful Rome is!" a boy exclaimed in the street.

Imperium Romanum ad maximas terras orbis terrarum extendit. "Imperium nostrum nunc amplissimum est," imperator Romanus in consilio militari dixit.

The Roman Empire extended to the greatest lands of the world. "Our empire is now the largest," a Roman emperor said in a military council.

Senatus Romanus in sapientia et prudentia crevit, rei publicae bene gerendae. "Senatus noster sapientissimus est," senator ad collegas suos dixit.

The Roman Senate grew in wisdom and prudence, governing the republic well. "Our Senate is the wisest," a senator said to his colleagues.

Romani historiam suam magnifice scribebant, gesta et victorias celebrantes. "Historiam nostram gloriose scribemus," scriptor in tablino suo dixit.

The Romans wrote their history magnificently, celebrating their deeds and victories. "We will write our history gloriously," a writer said in his study.

Roma aeterna, per saecula, in historia mundi manebat. "Roma aeterna est," civis Romanus in templum Iovis ingressus dixit.

Eternal Rome remained in the history of the world for centuries. "Rome is eternal," a Roman citizen said as he entered the temple of Jupiter.

Per saecula, civitas Romana in gloria et honore vixit. "Per saecula, gloria Romae vivet," poeta in theatro suo recitavit.

For centuries, the Roman city lived in glory and honor. "For centuries, the glory of Rome will live," a poet recited in his theater.

Roma, memoria et cultura sua, in memoriam mundi semper manet. "Roma in memoria mundi semper erit," peregrinus, urbem spectans, cogitavit.

Rome, with its memory and culture, always remains in the world's remembrance. "Rome will always be in the world's memory," a traveler thought as he gazed at the city.

Hoc capitulo, renovatio et exaltatio Romae post calamitatem Gallicam illustratur. Roma non solum urbs restituta sed etiam caput culturale et politicum mundi efficitur. Scientiae, artes, leges, et cultura Romana per totum orbem terrarum extenduntur, Romaque aeterna in historia humana manet.

In this chapter, the renewal and exaltation of Rome after the Gallic calamity is illustrated. Rome is not only restored as a city but also becomes the cultural and political capital of the world. Roman science, arts, laws, and culture spread throughout the world, and eternal Rome remains in human history.

Roma Invicta

Capitulum Primum: Hannibal Alpes Transgreditur

Hannibal, dux Carthaginiensis, Romam vincere constituit. "Romam vincere volo," Hannibal suis dixit.

Hannibal, the Carthaginian leader, decided to conquer Rome. "I want to conquer Rome," Hannibal said to his men.

Ex Hispania, Hannibal cum magno exercitu profectus est. "In Italiam ibimus," Hannibal militibus suis imperavit.

From Spain, Hannibal set out with a great army. "We will go to Italy," Hannibal ordered his soldiers.

Multos milites fortes et elephantes magnos secum duxit. "Milites et elephantes nobis victoriam ferent," Hannibal ad suos dixit.

He led many strong soldiers and large elephants with him. "The soldiers and elephants will bring us victory," Hannibal said to his men.

Decrevit Alpes, montes altos et nive plenos, transire. "Per Alpes ibimus," Hannibal consulibus suis explicavit.

He decided to cross the Alps, tall mountains full of snow. "We will go through the Alps," Hannibal explained to his officers.

Iter per Alpes difficile et plenum periculorum erat. "Hoc iter arduum est," miles Carthaginiensis in castris dixit.

The journey through the Alps was difficult and full of dangers. "This journey is arduous," a Carthaginian soldier said in the camp.

Romani de Hannibalis consilio audierunt et magnopere timuerunt. "Hannibal venit!" Romanus in foro clamavit.

The Romans heard of Hannibal's plan and were greatly afraid. "Hannibal is coming!" a Roman shouted in the forum.

Hannibal flumina, silvas, et altos montes superavit. "Nihil nos deterret," Hannibal ad milites suos in montibus dixit.

Hannibal overcame rivers, forests, and high mountains. "Nothing will deter us," Hannibal said to his soldiers in the mountains.

In via, multi milites et elephantes perierunt. "Difficile est, sed pergemus," dux Carthaginiensis ad suos dixit.

On the way, many soldiers and elephants perished. "It is difficult, but we will continue," the Carthaginian leader said to his men.

Elephantes, quamquam labore gravati, perseveraverunt. "Elephantes fortes sunt," Hannibal, montes aspiciens, inquit.

The elephants, though burdened by the effort, persevered. "The elephants are strong," Hannibal said, looking at the mountains.

Incolae montanorum, Hannibalem videntes, eum impedire conati sunt. "Hunc ducem arceamus!" incola montanus ad alios clamavit.

The mountain dwellers, seeing Hannibal, tried to stop him. "Let us block this leader!" a mountain dweller shouted to the others.

Hannibal, astutia et virtute usus, incolas superavit. "Astutia nostra nos servat," Hannibal ad legatum suum dixit.

Hannibal, using cunning and bravery, defeated the inhabitants. "Our cunning saves us," Hannibal said to his lieutenant.

Post multos dies laborum, Hannibal tandem Italiam attigit. "Italia nostra est!" Hannibal, terram novam aspiciens, exclamavit.

After many days of hardship, Hannibal finally reached Italy. "Italy is ours!" Hannibal exclaimed, gazing at the new land.

Exercitus Romanus, Hannibalis adventum audiens, ad eum oppugnandum parabat. "Hannibalem vincamus!" consul Romanus militibus suis imperavit.

The Roman army, hearing of Hannibal's arrival, prepared to attack him. "Let us defeat Hannibal!" the Roman consul ordered his soldiers.

Hannibal, in Italia, Romanos ad pugnam provocavit. "Romani, venite et pugnate!" Hannibal in campo clamavit.

In Italy, Hannibal challenged the Romans to fight. "Romans, come and fight!" Hannibal shouted on the battlefield.

Prima proelia inter Romanos et Hannibalem in Italia coeperunt. "Proelium incipit," miles Carthaginiensis, gladium stringens, dixit.

The first battles between the Romans and Hannibal began in Italy. "The battle begins," a Carthaginian soldier said, drawing his sword.

Capitulum Secundum: Proelium ad Ticinum

Hannibal, dux Carthaginiensis, Romanos ad flumen Ticinum oppugnavit. "Romanos ad Ticinum vincemus!" Hannibal suis militibus imperavit.

Hannibal, the Carthaginian leader, attacked the Romans at the River Ticinus. "We will defeat the Romans at Ticinus!" Hannibal ordered his soldiers.

Publius Cornelius Scipio, dux Romanorum, exercitum ad proelium duxit. "Contra Hannibalem pugnabimus," Scipio Romanis dixit.

Publius Cornelius Scipio, the Roman leader, led his army into battle. "We will fight against Hannibal," Scipio told the Romans.

Hannibal Romae terram et cives terrere voluit. "Terram Romanam territuri sumus," Hannibal astute cogitavit.

Hannibal wanted to terrify the land and citizens of Rome. "We will frighten Roman territory," Hannibal cunningly thought.

Proelium ad Ticinum durum et cruentum factum est. "Proelium incepit," miles Romanus in acie clamavit.

The battle at Ticinus was hard and bloody. "The battle has begun," a Roman soldier shouted in the battle line.

In proelio, Romanorum equites a Hannibale et eius equitibus superati sunt. "Hannibal nos vincit!" eques Romanus, fugiens, clamavit.

In the battle, the Roman cavalry were defeated by Hannibal and his horsemen. "Hannibal is defeating us!" a Roman cavalryman shouted as he fled.

Scipio, dux Romanorum, in proelio graviter vulneratus est. "Scipio vulneratus est!" nuntius ad alios Romanos dixit.

Scipio, the Roman leader, was gravely wounded in the battle. "Scipio is wounded!" a messenger told the other Romans.

Romani, clade affecti, se ad flumen Padum receperunt. "Ad Padum fugiamus!" centurio Romanus suis militibus imperavit.

The Romans, affected by the defeat, retreated to the River Po. "Let us flee to the Po!" a Roman centurion ordered his soldiers.

Hannibal, proelio ad Ticinum victo, victoriam parvam reportavit. "Victoria nostra est!" Hannibal, triumphans, exclamavit.

Hannibal, having won the battle at Ticinus, gained a small victory. "Victory is ours!" Hannibal exclaimed triumphantly.

Animi Romanorum a proelio fracti sunt, timore et desperatione affecti. "Quid faciemus?" Romanus, trepidus, in castris rogavit.

The spirits of the Romans were broken by the battle, filled with fear and despair. "What will we do?" a fearful Roman asked in the camp.

Hannibal, victoria ad Ticinum laetus, ad ulteriores victorias in Italia movebat. "Italiam vincemus!" Hannibal suis dixit.

Hannibal, pleased with the victory at Ticinus, moved toward further victories in Italy. "We will conquer Italy!" Hannibal told his men.

Romani, duce vulnerato, novum consulem eligere debebant. "Novum ducem eligere debemus," senator Romanus in senatu dixit.

The Romans, with their leader wounded, had to elect a new consul. "We must choose a new leader," a Roman senator said in the Senate.

Hannibal, Romanorum terrorem augere cupiens, strategiam novam cogitavit. "Romanos terrebimus," Hannibal ad consilium suum dixit.

Hannibal, wishing to increase the Romans' fear, devised a new strategy. "We will terrify the Romans," Hannibal told his council.

Romani, de nova strategia ad Hannibalem vincendum cogitabant. "Strategiam novam invenire debemus," consul Romanus alteri consuli dixit.

The Romans were thinking of a new strategy to defeat Hannibal. "We must find a new strategy," one Roman consul said to the other.

Nuntii de proelio ad Ticinum per Italiam diffusi sunt, timorem per civitates spargentes. "Hannibal vicimus!" nuntius in urbe clamavit.

News of the battle at Ticinus spread through Italy, spreading fear among the cities. "Hannibal has won!" a messenger shouted in the city.

Timor et sollicitudo in civitate Romana creverunt, futurum incertum considerantes. "Quid futurum est?" civis Romanus, sollicitus, in foro rogavit.

Fear and anxiety grew in the Roman state as they considered the uncertain future. "What will happen?" a worried Roman citizen asked in the forum.

In hoc capitulo, descriptio est proelii ad Ticinum, ubi Hannibal primam victoriam contra Romanos reportavit. Dux Romanus vulneratus est, et Romanorum animi fracti sunt, dum Hannibal ad ulteriores actiones in Italia movebat. Romanorum timor et incertitudo de futuro bello contra Carthaginem crevit.

In this chapter, the battle at Ticinus is described, where Hannibal won his first victory against the Romans. The Roman leader was wounded, and the Romans' spirits were broken as Hannibal moved toward further actions in Italy. Roman fear and uncertainty about the future war with Carthage grew.

Capitulum Tertium: Proelium ad Trebiam

Tiberius Sempronius Longus, consul Romanus novus, cum exercitu suo ad Trebiam flumen venit. "Ad Trebiam procedemus," in castris Romanis dixit.

Tiberius Sempronius Longus, the new Roman consul, came with his army to the River Trebia. "We will advance to Trebia," he said in the Roman camp.

Hannibal, dux Carthaginiensis, Romanos ad proelium ad Trebiam provocavit. "Romanos ad Trebiam vincemus," Hannibal suis militibus imperavit.

Hannibal, the Carthaginian leader, challenged the Romans to battle at Trebia. "We will defeat the Romans at Trebia," Hannibal ordered his soldiers.

Exercitus Romanorum ad pugnam contra Hannibalem paratus erat. "Parati ad pugnam sumus," Tiberius Sempronius Longus militibus suis dixit.

The Roman army was prepared for battle against Hannibal. "We are ready for battle," Tiberius Sempronius Longus said to his soldiers.

Hannibal, astutia sua notus, Romanos ad Trebiam decipere conatus est. "Astutia victoriam nobis dabit," Hannibal cogitavit.

Hannibal, known for his cunning, attempted to deceive the Romans at Trebia. "Cunning will give us victory," Hannibal thought.

Proelium mane coepit, aqua gelida fluminis Trebiae Romanos impediente. "Aqua frigida est," miles Romanus, trepidans, inquit.

The battle began in the morning, with the cold waters of the River Trebia hindering the Romans. "The water is freezing," a trembling Roman soldier said.

Romani et Carthaginienses in proelio Trebiae fortiter pugnaverunt. "Pro Roma!" Romani, pugnantes, clamaverunt.

The Romans and Carthaginians fought fiercely in the battle at Trebia. "For Rome!" the Romans shouted as they fought.

Equites Romani in difficili loco erant, hostium impetibus prementibus. "Pressi sumus," eques Romanus ad alium dixit.

The Roman cavalry were in a difficult position, overwhelmed by the enemy's attacks. "We are under pressure," one Roman cavalryman said to another.

Hannibal elephantis et peditibus in proelio usus est. "Elephantes et pedites in pugnam ducite," Hannibal imperavit.

Hannibal used elephants and infantry in the battle. "Lead the elephants and infantry into the fight," Hannibal ordered.

Proelium multa confusione plenum erat, Romanos et Carthaginienses in misso pugnantes. "Confusio est," miles Romanus in tumultu dixit.

The battle was full of confusion, with Romans and Carthaginians fighting in disorder. "There is chaos," a Roman soldier said in the turmoil.

Exercitus Romanorum in proelio graviter pressus est, Hannibalis copiis valentibus. "Pressi sumus," centurio Romanus exclamavit.

The Roman army was heavily pressed in the battle, as Hannibal's forces were strong. "We are under pressure," a Roman centurion exclaimed.

Hannibal, proelio ad Trebiam gesto, claram victoriam reportavit. "Victoria nostra est," Hannibal, laetus, dixit.

Hannibal, having fought the battle at Trebia, claimed a decisive victory. "Victory is ours," Hannibal said happily.

Romani in proelio ad Trebiam multos milites amiserunt, campo pugnae sanguine tincto. "Amisimus multos," Tiberius Sempronius Longus maestus inquit.

The Romans lost many soldiers in the battle at Trebia, with the battlefield stained with blood. "We have lost many," Tiberius Sempronius Longus said sadly.

Tiberius Sempronius Longus, clade accepta, se cum reliquis Romanis ad urbes proximas recepit. "Ad urbes proximas recedamus," consul Romanus dixit.

Tiberius Sempronius Longus, having suffered defeat, withdrew with the remaining Romans to nearby cities. "Let us retreat to the nearby cities," the Roman consul said.

Post victoriam ad Trebiam, Hannibal Italiam ulterius invadebat, Romanos terrens. "Italiam capiemus," Hannibal suis dixit.

After the victory at Trebia, Hannibal continued his invasion of Italy, frightening the Romans. "We will take Italy," Hannibal told his men.

Romani, de Hannibalis victoriis ad Trebiam audientes, territi erant. "Quid nunc faciemus?" senator Romanus in senatu rogavit.

The Romans, hearing of Hannibal's victories at Trebia, were terrified. "What shall we do now?" a Roman senator asked in the Senate.

In hoc capitulo, proelium ad Trebiam inter Romanos et Carthaginienses sub Hannibale descriptum est. Exercitus Romanus graviter pressus est, et clara victoria ad Hannibalem pervenit. Romanorum timor et sollicitudo de futuro bello contra Hannibalem et Carthaginienses crescebant.

In this chapter, the battle at Trebia between the Romans and the Carthaginians under Hannibal is described. The Roman army was heavily pressed, and a clear victory went to Hannibal. The Romans' fear and concern about the future war against Hannibal and the Carthaginians were growing.

Capitulum Quartum: Proelium ad Trasumennum

Hannibal, dux astutus Carthaginiensis, Romanos ad lacum Trasumennum insidias paravit. "Insidias Romanis parabimus," Hannibal suis militibus imperavit.

Hannibal, the cunning Carthaginian leader, prepared an ambush for the Romans at Lake Trasimene. "We will set a trap for the Romans," Hannibal ordered his soldiers.

Gaius Flaminius, consul Romanorum, Hannibalem per Italiam secutus est. "Hannibalem insequemur," Flaminius suis dixit.

Gaius Flaminius, the Roman consul, followed Hannibal through Italy. "We will pursue Hannibal," Flaminius told his men.

Hannibal Romanos in vallem angustam et periculosam duxit. "In hanc vallem eos inducemus," Hannibal, callidus, cogitavit.

Hannibal led the Romans into a narrow and dangerous valley. "We will lure them into this valley," Hannibal, cunning, thought.

Romanorum exercitus, Flamini duce, in Hannibalis insidias incidit. "In insidias incidimus!" miles Romanus, territus, exclamavit.

The Roman army, led by Flaminius, fell into Hannibal's ambush. "We have fallen into a trap!" a terrified Roman soldier exclaimed.

Proelium in loco difficili et angusto coepit. "Pugnate!" Flaminius Romanis imperavit.

The battle began in a difficult and narrow place. "Fight!" Flaminius ordered the Romans.

Ordines Romanorum a Carthaginiensibus circumventi sunt, pugna aspera exorto. "Circumventi sumus," Romanus in proelio dixit.

The Roman ranks were surrounded by the Carthaginians as a fierce battle broke out. "We are surrounded," a Roman said in the battle.

Pugna aspera et confusa in vallibus et collibus Trasumeni erat. "Confusi sumus," Romanus in tumultu pugnae inquit.

The battle was fierce and chaotic in the valleys and hills of Trasimene. "We are confused," a Roman said in the turmoil of the battle.

Gaius Flaminius, consul Romanorum, in proelio fortiter pugnans, occisus est. "Consul cecidit!" Romanus, luctu affectus, clamavit.

Gaius Flaminius, the Roman consul, was killed while fighting bravely in the battle. "The consul has fallen!" a Roman, overcome with grief, shouted.

Romani in proelio ad Trasumennum gravem cladem acceperunt. "Victi sumus," Romanus, fugiens, dixit.

The Romans suffered a heavy defeat in the battle at Trasimene. "We are defeated," a fleeing Roman said.

Hannibal, victoria ad Trasumennum reportata, laetus erat. "Victoriam magnam habemus," Hannibal ad milites suos dixit.

Hannibal, having won the victory at Trasimene, was joyful. "We have a great victory," Hannibal told his soldiers.

Romani, clade accepta, de novo consule et novis copiis cogitabant. "Novum ducem eligere debemus," senator Romanus in senatu dixit.

The Romans, having suffered defeat, were thinking about a new consul and new troops. "We must choose a new leader," a Roman senator said in the Senate.

Nuntii de clade ad Trasumennum Romam pervenerunt, civitatem in luctum deducentes. "Cladem accepimus," nuntius in foro Romano dixit.

The news of the defeat at Trasimene reached Rome, plunging the city into mourning. "We have suffered a defeat," a messenger said in the Roman forum.

Senatus Romanus, audita clade, magnam sollicitudinem habuit. "Quid agemus?" senator alio senatori rogavit.

The Roman Senate, having heard of the defeat, was deeply concerned. "What will we do?" one senator asked another.

Hannibal, victoria sua fretus, per Italiam sine magna resistentia movebat. "Italiam capiemus," Hannibal, confidens, suis dixit.

Hannibal, relying on his victory, moved through Italy with little resistance. "We will capture Italy," Hannibal confidently told his men.

Timor et sollicitudo in Romanis augebantur, futuro incerto. "Quid futurum est?" civis Romanus, sollicitus, in via Romae rogavit.

Fear and anxiety were growing among the Romans, with the future uncertain. "What will happen?" a worried Roman citizen asked in the streets of Rome.

In hoc capitulo, descriptio est proelii ad Trasumennum, ubi Hannibal Romanos in insidias duxit et gravem cladem eis intulit. Gaius Flaminius, consul, in proelio occisus est, et Romanorum exercitus magnam cladem accepit, quae Romanorum timorem et sollicitudinem de futuro bello contra Hannibalem et Carthaginienses auget.

In this chapter, the battle at Trasimene is described, where Hannibal led the Romans into an ambush and inflicted a heavy defeat upon them. Gaius Flaminius, the consul, was killed in the battle, and the Roman army suffered a great loss, increasing the Romans' fear and anxiety about the future war against Hannibal and the Carthaginians.

Capitulum Quintum: Proelium ad Cannas

Lucius Aemilius Paullus et Gaius Terentius Varro, consules novi Romanorum, Hannibalem ad Cannas oppugnare constituerunt. "Ad Cannas procedemus," Lucius Aemilius Paullus in consilio dixit.

Lucius Aemilius Paullus and Gaius Terentius Varro, the new Roman consuls, decided to attack Hannibal at Cannae. "We will advance to Cannae," Lucius Aemilius Paullus said in the council.

Hannibal, dux Carthaginiensis, consilium audax ad proelium Cannense paravit. "Strategiam nostram adhibebimus," Hannibal suis militibus imperavit.

Hannibal, the Carthaginian leader, prepared a bold plan for the Battle of Cannae. "We will use our strategy," Hannibal ordered his soldiers.

Exercitus Romanorum maximus proelio ad Cannas congregatus est. "Exercitum maximum habemus," Gaius Terentius Varro dixit.

The largest Roman army gathered for battle at Cannae. "We have the largest army," Gaius Terentius Varro said.

Proelium in campis Cannensibus coepit, sol ardens et pulvis in aere. "Proelium incipit," miles Romanus in acie clamavit.

The battle began on the plains of Cannae, with the sun blazing and dust in the air. "The battle begins," a Roman soldier shouted in the ranks.

Hannibal arte militari Romanorum ordines circumvenit. "Romanos circumveniemus," Hannibal, callidus, in proelio dixit.

Hannibal used military skill to surround the Roman ranks. "We will surround the Romans," Hannibal said cunningly during the battle.

Pugna ad Cannas cruenta et difficilis erat, milites utrimque fortiter pugnantes. "Pugnate fortes!" Lucius Aemilius Paullus Romanis imperavit.

The battle at Cannae was bloody and difficult, with soldiers on both sides fighting bravely. "Fight bravely!" Lucius Aemilius Paullus commanded the Romans.

Romanorum milites, quamquam fortiter pugnantes, in difficultate erant. "Difficile est," miles Romanus, luctans, inquit.

The Roman soldiers, although fighting bravely, were in trouble. "This is difficult," a struggling Roman soldier said.

Hannibal peditibus et equitibus in proelio bene usus est, Romanos premens. "Pedites et equites in pugnam ducite," Hannibal, tactico, suis dixit.

Hannibal used both infantry and cavalry effectively in the battle, putting pressure on the Romans. "Lead the infantry and cavalry into the fight," Hannibal tactically instructed his men.

Romanorum exercitus, a Carthaginiensibus circumventus, in magno periculo erat. "Circumventi sumus!" Romanus in proelio exclamavit.

The Roman army, surrounded by the Carthaginians, was in great danger. "We are surrounded!" a Roman shouted in the battle.

Lucius Aemilius Paullus, consul, in proelio a Carthaginiensibus occisus est. "Consul cecidit!" Romanus, territus, clamavit.

Lucius Aemilius Paullus, the consul, was killed in the battle by the Carthaginians. "The consul has fallen!" a terrified Roman shouted.

Clades Romana ad Cannas maxima fuit, multos milites amittentes. "Amisimus," Romanus superstitus dixit.

The Roman defeat at Cannae was massive, with many soldiers lost. "We have lost," a surviving Roman said.

Hannibal, proelio Cannensi victo, victoriam ingentem reportavit. "Victoria magna est nostra," Hannibal ad milites suos dixit.

Hannibal, having won the Battle of Cannae, achieved an enormous victory. "The great victory is ours," Hannibal told his soldiers.

Romani, clade Cannensi accepta, de summa desperatione cogitaverunt. "Quid faciemus?" senator Romanus in senatu rogavit.

The Romans, having suffered the defeat at Cannae, thought about their extreme despair. "What will we do?" a Roman senator asked in the Senate.

Roma, post cladem Cannensem, auxilium et salutem quaerebat. "Auxilium nobis opus est," civis Romanus in foro dixit.

Rome, after the defeat at Cannae, sought help and safety. "We need help," a Roman citizen said in the forum.

Hannibal, post victoriam ad Cannas, Romanorum timorem et terrorem maxime augit. "Romanos terrebimus," Hannibal, victor, cogitavit.

Hannibal, after the victory at Cannae, greatly increased the Romans' fear and terror. "We will terrify the Romans," Hannibal, triumphant, thought.

In hoc capitulo, descriptio est proelii ad Cannas, ubi Hannibal, dux Carthaginiensis, maximam victoriam contra Romanos reportavit. Consul Romanus in proelio cecidit, et Romanorum exercitus gravi clade affectus est, quae Romanorum timorem et desperationem de futuro bello contra Hannibalem et Carthaginienses magnopere augit.

In this chapter, the Battle of Cannae is described, where Hannibal, the Carthaginian leader, won a great victory against the Romans. The Roman consul fell in the battle, and the Roman army was severely defeated, which greatly increased the Romans' fear and despair regarding the future war against Hannibal and the Carthaginians.

Capitulum Sextum: Roma Resurgit

Post graves clades acceptas, Romani novas vires et animos collegerunt. "Novam fortitudinem inveniemus," senator Romanus in senatu dixit.

After suffering heavy defeats, the Romans gathered new strength and courage. "We will find new strength," a Roman senator said in the Senate.

Publius Cornelius Scipio Africanus, vir iuvenis et audax, dux Romanorum novus electus est. "Scipionem ducem faciemus," populus in comitiis clamavit.

Publius Cornelius Scipio Africanus, a young and bold man, was elected as the new leader of the Romans. "We will make Scipio our leader," the people shouted in the assembly.

Scipio novas tacticas militares et disciplinam in exercitu Romanorum adhibuit. "Novam disciplinam militarem adhibebimus," Scipio suis militibus in castris dixit.

Scipio introduced new military tactics and discipline in the Roman army. "We will apply new military discipline," Scipio said to his soldiers in the camp.

Virtus et fortitudo in exercitu Romano renovatae sunt. "Fortiores sumus," miles Romanus ad commilitonem suum in exercitu dixit.

The courage and strength of the Roman army were renewed. "We are stronger," a Roman soldier said to his comrade in the army.

Scipio in Hispaniam missus est, Carthaginienses ibi oppugnaturus. "Hispaniam liberabimus," Scipio, navigans, cogitavit.

Scipio was sent to Spain to attack the Carthaginians there. "We will liberate Spain," Scipio thought as he sailed.

In Hispania, Scipio Carthaginienses multa proelia vicit. "Victoriam reportavimus!" nuntius ad Romam rettulit.

In Spain, Scipio won many battles against the Carthaginians. "We have achieved victory!" a messenger reported back to Rome.

Romani, Scipionis victoriis in Hispania auditis, fiduciam recuperaverunt. "Scipio nos ad victoriam ducit," civis Romanus in foro dixit.

The Romans, having heard of Scipio's victories in Spain, regained their confidence. "Scipio is leading us to victory," a Roman citizen said in the forum.

Scipio deinde in Africam transiit, bellum directe ad Carthaginienses portans. "In Africam ibimus," Scipio ad milites suos in nave dixit.

Scipio then crossed into Africa, bringing the war directly to the Carthaginians. "We will go to Africa," Scipio said to his soldiers on the ship.

Carthaginienses, Scipionis adventu in Africa cognito, de defensione cogitabant. "Romani in terram nostram venerunt," Carthaginiensis in senatu dixit.

The Carthaginians, learning of Scipio's arrival in Africa, were thinking about their defense. "The Romans have come to our land," a Carthaginian said in the Senate.

Scipio Romanos ad ultimam et decisivam victoriam in Africa ducebat. "Ad ultimam pugnam procedemus," Scipio, castra ponens, dixit.

Scipio was leading the Romans to their final and decisive victory in Africa. "We will proceed to the final battle," Scipio said as he set up camp.

Exercitus Romanus in Africa fortiter pugnavit, hostium copias premens. "Pro Roma pugnamus!" miles Romanus in proelio clamavit.

The Roman army fought bravely in Africa, pressing the enemy's forces. "We fight for Rome!" a Roman soldier shouted in the battle.

Sub Scipione, Roma iterum in arte bellica excellebat. "Arte nostra militari praevalere possumus," legatus Romanus ad alios duces dixit.

Under Scipio, Rome once again excelled in the art of war. "We can prevail with our military skill," a Roman officer said to other commanders.

Carthaginienses, pressi a Romanis, ad pacem petendam coacti sunt. "Pacem cum Romanis facere debemus," Carthaginiensis senator alteri senatori suadebat.

The Carthaginians, pressed by the Romans, were forced to seek peace. "We must make peace with the Romans," one Carthaginian senator urged another.

Romani, de ultima victoria in Africa cogitantes, spem magnam habebant. "Victoria nostra prope est," Romanus in foro cum amico suo colloquebatur.

The Romans, thinking about the final victory in Africa, had great hope. "Our victory is near," a Roman was saying to his friend in the forum.

Roma, ad ultimum triumphum contra Carthaginienses parabatur. "Triumphum parabimus," civis Romanus, exspectans, in urbe dixit.

Rome was preparing for the final triumph against the Carthaginians. "We will prepare for the triumph," a Roman citizen said, waiting in the city.

In hoc capitulo, restitutio et resurgentia Romana post clades Cannenses et Trasumeni descripta sunt. Sub ducatu Scipionis Africani, Romani novas vires et fortitudinem inveniunt, victorias in Hispania consequuntur, et bellum in Africam, patriam Carthaginiensium, portant. Spes Romana de ultima victoria et triumpho contra Carthaginem augescit.

In this chapter, the restoration and resurgence of Rome after the defeats at Cannae and Trasimene are described. Under the leadership of Scipio Africanus, the Romans find new strength and courage, achieve victories in Spain, and bring the war to Africa, the homeland of the Carthaginians. Roman hope for final victory and triumph against Carthage is growing.

Capitulum Septimum: Proelium ad Zamam

Scipio Africanus et Hannibal, duces magni, ad Zamam pugnaverunt. "Hodie cum Hannibale pugnabimus," Scipio suis dixit.

Scipio Africanus and Hannibal, great leaders, fought at Zama. "Today we will fight against Hannibal," Scipio said to his men.

Exercitus Romanorum et Carthaginiensium in campo prope Zamam steterunt, aciem parantes. "Exercitus paratus est," miles Romanus ad alium dixit.

The Roman and Carthaginian armies stood in the field near Zama, preparing their lines. "The army is ready," a Roman soldier said to another.

Proelium ad Zamam magnum et decisivum erat, futurum utriusque civitatis decernens. "Hoc proelium futurum nostrum decernet," Hannibal suis militibus inquit.

The battle at Zama was great and decisive, determining the future of both nations. "This battle will decide our future," Hannibal said to his soldiers.

Scipio, dux prudens, ordines Romanorum in campo bene disposuit. "Ordines nostros bene disponamus," Scipio strategice dixit.

Scipio, a wise leader, arranged the Roman ranks well in the field. "Let us arrange our ranks well," Scipio said strategically.

Hannibal elephantis, animalibus magnis et terribilibus, in proelio usus est. "Elephantes in prima acie ponite," Hannibal imperavit.

Hannibal used elephants, large and terrifying animals, in the battle. "Place the elephants in the front line," Hannibal ordered.

Exercitus Romanus, non territus, fortiter contra elephantes et Carthaginienses resistit. "Fortiter resistamus!" centurio Romanus suis clamavit.

The Roman army, undeterred, resisted bravely against the elephants and Carthaginians. "Let us resist bravely!" a Roman centurion shouted to his men.

Pugna ad Zamam diu et acriter gesta est, gladiis et clamoribus resonans. "Pugnate!" Hannibal in medio proelii clamavit.

The battle at Zama was fought long and fiercely, echoing with swords and shouts. "Fight!" Hannibal shouted in the midst of the battle.

Tacticae Romanorum, bene dispositae, Hannibalem et Carthaginienses superaverunt. "Tacticae nostrae efficaces sunt," Scipio, pugnam inspiciens, dixit.

The Roman tactics, well executed, overcame Hannibal and the Carthaginians. "Our tactics are effective," Scipio said, observing the battle.

Hannibal in proelio pressus est, Romanorum impetum sustinere non potens. "Pressi sumus," Hannibal, difficultate affectus, inquit.

Hannibal was pressed in the battle, unable to withstand the Roman attack. "We are under pressure," Hannibal said, struggling.

Scipio ad Zamam victoriam magnam reportavit, hostes superans. "Victoriam magnam reportavimus!" Scipio, laetus, exclamavit.

Scipio won a great victory at Zama, defeating the enemy. "We have achieved a great victory!" Scipio exclaimed happily.

Carthago, proelio Zamensi amissa, pacem cum Roma fecit. "Pacem facere debemus," senator Carthaginiensis dixit.

Carthage, having lost the Battle of Zama, made peace with Rome. "We must make peace," a Carthaginian senator said.

Roma, victoria Zamensi, super Carthaginem triumphavit. "Carthaginem vicimus!" populus Romanus in urbe exsultavit.

Rome, with the victory at Zama, triumphed over Carthage. "We have defeated Carthage!" the Roman people rejoiced in the city.

Scipio, propter victoriam Zamensem, 'Magnus' appellatus est, honor magnus. "Scipio Africanus Magnus est," Romanus in foro dixit.

Scipio, because of the victory at Zama, was called 'The Great,' a great honor. "Scipio Africanus is the Great," a Roman said in the forum.

Romani, pace facta et gloria assecuta, gaudebant. "Pace et gloria fruimur," civis Romanus ad amicum suum in foro dixit.

The Romans, having made peace and achieved glory, were rejoicing. "We are enjoying peace and glory," a Roman citizen said to his friend in the forum.

Carthago, victa, sub potestate Romana erat, finem belli significans. "Carthago nunc Romae est," Romanus, victoria contentus, in via dixit.

Carthage, having been defeated, was now under Roman control, signifying the end of the war. "Carthage now belongs to Rome," a content Roman said in the street.

Hoc capitulo, narratur proelium decisivum ad Zamam inter Romanos et Carthaginienses, ubi Scipio Africanus Magnus et Hannibal pugnaverunt. Romanorum victoria, tacticae efficaces, et fortitudo in proelio ad Zamam claram victoriam Romanis attulerunt, quae pacem et dominationem Romae in regione Mediterranea confirmavit. Carthago pacem cum Roma fecit, et Scipio ob victoriam suam celebratus est.

In this chapter, the decisive Battle of Zama between the Romans and Carthaginians is narrated, where Scipio Africanus the Great and Hannibal fought. The Roman victory, through effective tactics and bravery in the battle at Zama, brought a clear victory to the Romans, confirming peace and Roman dominance in the Mediterranean region. Carthage made peace with Rome, and Scipio was celebrated for his victory.

Capitulum Octavum: Pax et Gloria Romae

Post bellum cum Carthagine, pax inter Romanos et Carthaginienses facta est. "Pacem cum Carthagine fecimus," senator Romanus in senatu dixit.

After the war with Carthage, peace was made between the Romans and the Carthaginians. "We have made peace with Carthage," a Roman senator said in the Senate.

Roma potestatem suam in Mediterraneo mari confirmavit, dominium augens. "Mare nostrum est," Romanus ad portum dixit.

Rome confirmed its power in the Mediterranean Sea, increasing its dominion. "The sea is ours," a Roman said at the port.

Scipio Africanus, dux victoriosus, ut heros Romanus celebratus est. "Scipio heros noster est," civis Romanus in foro exclamavit.

Scipio Africanus, the victorious leader, was celebrated as a Roman hero. "Scipio is our hero," a Roman citizen exclaimed in the forum.

Romani vias, portus, et urbes per imperium aedificaverunt, infrastructuram augentes. "Vias et urbes aedificamus," architectus Romanus in officina sua dixit.

The Romans built roads, ports, and cities throughout the empire, increasing infrastructure. "We are building roads and cities," a Roman architect said in his workshop.

Commercium et cultura Romana floruerunt, opulentia et sapientia crescentes. "Commercium nostrum floret," mercator Romanus in emporio suo dixit.

Roman trade and culture flourished, with wealth and knowledge growing. "Our trade is thriving," a Roman merchant said in his shop.

Roma leges et iustitiam non solum intra muros suos sed etiam gentibus externis dedit. "Leges nostrae iustitiae sunt," iurisconsultus Romanus in curia dixit.

Rome gave laws and justice not only within its walls but also to foreign nations. "Our laws are just," a Roman jurist said in the courthouse.

Exemplar Romae per orbem terrarum imitatum est, civitates aliae Romanam culturam et leges sequentes. "Exemplar Romae ubique est," peregrinus in Roma dixit.

The example of Rome was imitated throughout the world, with other cities following Roman culture and laws. "Rome's example is everywhere," a foreigner said in Rome.

Pax Romana, a Romanis stabilita, per longum tempus in imperio manebat. "Pax nostra longa est," matrona Romana in domo sua dixit.

The Pax Romana, established by the Romans, lasted for a long time in the empire. "Our peace is enduring," a Roman matron said in her home.

Imperium Romanorum ad novas terras et populos extendebatur, imperium augens. "Terras novas habemus," explorator Romanus ad collegam suum dixit.

The Roman Empire extended to new lands and peoples, increasing its power. "We have new lands," a Roman explorer said to his colleague.

Roma, urbs pulchra et potens, ab omnibus admirabatur, magnitudine et pulchritudine eius. "Quam pulchra est Roma!" peregrinus in via Romana admirans dixit.

Rome, a beautiful and powerful city, was admired by all for its size and beauty. "How beautiful Rome is!" a traveler, admiring, said in a Roman street.

In artibus et scientiis Romani excellebant, novas inventiones et opera creantes. "In artibus et scientiis excelsi sumus," artifex Romanus in studio suo dixit.

The Romans excelled in the arts and sciences, creating new inventions and works. "We excel in the arts and sciences," a Roman artist said in his studio.

Roma caput mundi facta est, locus artium et rerum gestarum princeps orbis terrarum. "Roma caput mundi est," magister in schola Romana discipulis suis dixit.

Rome became the capital of the world, the chief place of arts and achievements. "Rome is the capital of the world," a teacher said to his students in a Roman school.

Gloria Romanorum in historia perpetua erat, facta eorum in annalibus et libris scripta. "Gloria nostra in historia manebit," scriptor Romanus in bibliotheca sua scribebat.

The glory of the Romans was everlasting in history, with their deeds written in annals and books. "Our glory will remain in history," a Roman writer said in his library.

Roma aeternitatem in cultu et historia assecuta est, memoria eius per saecula durans. "Roma aeterna est," sacerdos Romanus in templo dixit.

Rome achieved eternity in culture and history, with its memory lasting through the ages. "Rome is eternal," a Roman priest said in the temple.

Roma, magna et gloriosa, in memoriam aeternam manet, exemplum potentiae et culturæ. "Roma in aeternum manebit," senator Romanus in concilio dixit.

Rome, great and glorious, remains in eternal memory, an example of power and culture. "Rome will remain forever," a Roman senator said in the council.

Hoc capitulo, pax et gloria Romae post secundum bellum Punicum describuntur. Roma, victoria Scipionis freta, suam potentiam et culturam per Mediterraneum et ultra expandit, exemplar civitatis et potentiae globalis facta. Pax Romana stabilita est, et Roma in historia humana ut civitas magna et gloriosa manet.

In this chapter, the peace and glory of Rome after the Second Punic War are described. Relying on Scipio's victory, Rome expanded its power and culture throughout the Mediterranean and beyond, becoming a global example of statehood and power. The

Pax Romana was established, and Rome remains in human history as a great and glorious city.

Res Gestae Caesaris: A Roma ad Africam

Capitulum Primum: Caesar in Africa

Julius Caesar, magnus dux Romanorum, cum exercitu suo in Africam venit. Multos milites fortissimos secum ducit. Omnes parati sunt ad bellum gerendum.

Julius Caesar, the great leader of the Romans, came into Africa with his army. He brought many of the bravest soldiers with him. All are ready for war.

Terra Africana arida et calida est, sed milites Romani fortes et audaces sunt.

The African land is dry and hot, but the Roman soldiers are strong and brave.

"Ecce Africa! Terra plena periculis," dicit Caesar, oculis in horizontem fixis. "Parati ad bellum sumus," respondet centurio, gladium suum stringens.

"Behold Africa! A land full of dangers," says Caesar, his eyes fixed on the horizon. "We are ready for war," responds the centurion, drawing his sword.

Castra prope litus maris statuuntur. Tentoria et vallum celeriter aedificantur. "Exploratores, ite et hostium loca invenite," Caesar imperat. Exploratores, leves et celeres, in tenebras noctis discedunt.

The camp is set up near the sea. Tents and a rampart are quickly built. "Scouts, go and find the enemy positions," Caesar commands. The scouts, swift and light, disappear into the night's darkness.

Noctu, castra silenta sunt. Milites, lassi post longum iter, in tentoriis dormiunt. Caesar in tabernaculo suo cogitat. Bellum contra Scipionem, fortissimum ducem hostium, non facile erit.

At night, the camp is silent. The soldiers, weary after a long journey, sleep in their tents. Caesar thinks in his tent. The war against Scipio, the strongest enemy leader, will not be easy.

Subito, Caesar somnium habet. In somnio, Victoria, dea victoriae, apparet et dicit, "Caesar, tibi victoriam dabo." Caesar, somnio excitatus, spe plenus fit.

Suddenly, Caesar has a dream. In the dream, Victoria, the goddess of victory, appears and says, "Caesar, I will give you victory." Caesar, awakened by the dream, becomes full of hope.

Prima luce, tubae sonant. Signum est ad milites surgendi. "Milites, surgite! Parati ad pugnam estote!" centurio clamat. Milites cito armantur, gladiis et scutis suis.

At dawn, the trumpets sound. It is the signal for the soldiers to rise. "Soldiers, get up! Be ready for battle!" the centurion shouts. The soldiers quickly arm themselves with their swords and shields.

Caesar ante milites stat et eos fortiter adhortatur. "Hodie, fortitudinem et virtutem nostram ostendemus. Pro Roma et gloria pugnabimus!" Caesar exclamat.

Caesar stands before the soldiers and encourages them boldly. "Today, we will show our strength and courage. We will fight for Rome and glory!" Caesar exclaims.

Milites, virtute et spe pleni, exclamant, "Pro Caesar! Pro Roma!" Pugnae parati, in aciem procedunt, Caesar duce eorum.

The soldiers, full of courage and hope, shout, "For Caesar! For Rome!" Ready for battle, they march into formation, with Caesar leading them.

Et sic, cum prima luce, Caesar et eius milites ad novum diem et novas pugnas in Africa parati sunt, spe victoriae in cordibus eorum ardentibus.

And so, at first light, Caesar and his soldiers are ready for a new day and new battles in Africa, with the hope of victory burning in their hearts.

Capitulum Secundum: Preparatio ad Pugnam

In luce matutina, nuntius ad Caesarem venit. "Exercitus Scipionis appropinquat," nuntiat. Caesar, sine timore, copias suas disponit.

In the morning light, a messenger came to Caesar. "Scipio's army is approaching," he announced. Caesar, without fear, arranged his forces.

"Equites, vos in fronte collocate," Caesar equitibus imperat. Equites, veloces et fortes, locum suum in acie capiunt.

"Calvary, position yourselves at the front," Caesar commanded the cavalry. The cavalry, swift and strong, took their place in the line.

Post equites, pedites ordinantur. "Pedites, vos post equites sistite," imperat Caesar. Pedites, scutis et gladiis armati, obedientes stant.

Behind the cavalry, the infantry were arranged. "Infantry, stand behind the cavalry," Caesar ordered. The infantry, armed with shields and swords, obediently stood.

Inter pedites, sagittarii locantur. "Sagittarii, vos inter pedites ponite," Caesar dicit. Sagittarii, sagittis parati, locum suum inveniunt.

Among the infantry, the archers were placed. "Archers, position yourselves among the infantry," Caesar said. The archers, ready with their arrows, found their place.

Milites omnes, scutis et gladiis armati, parati ad pugnam sunt. Caesar, imperator fortis, omnibus imperat.

All the soldiers, armed with shields and swords, were ready for battle. Caesar, the brave commander, gave orders to all.

In acie, milites signum proelii exspectant. Tensio et expectatio in aere sunt. Omnes silent et ventum audire possunt.

In the battle line, the soldiers waited for the signal to fight. Tension and expectation filled the air. Everyone was silent, and they could hear the wind.

Scipio, dux hostium, suos milites adhortatur. "Hodie, pro libertate et patria pugnabimus!" clamat. Milites Scipionis clamant et gladios in aere movent.

Scipio, the enemy leader, encouraged his soldiers. "Today, we will fight for freedom and country!" he shouted. Scipio's soldiers shouted and raised their swords in the air.

Subito, tubae sonant. Signum pugnae datum est. Equites Romani primum impetum faciunt. Equis suis vehementer incitatis, in hostes ruunt.

Suddenly, the trumpets sounded. The signal for battle was given. The Roman cavalry made the first charge. Urging their horses forward fiercely, they rushed at the enemy.

Post equites, pedites Romani subsequuntur. Fortiter et celeriter procedunt, scutis et gladiis in hostes directis.

Behind the cavalry, the Roman infantry followed. They advanced bravely and quickly, directing their shields and swords at the enemy.

Sagittarii, in acie stantes, sagittas in hostes mittunt. Sagittae per aera volant et in hostium scuta et corpora cadunt.

The archers, standing in formation, shot arrows at the enemy. Arrows flew through the air and struck the shields and bodies of the enemy.

Et sic, pugna incipit. Exercitus Romanus et exercitus Scipionis in campo Africano conveniunt. Clamor, strepitus, et sonus armorum omnia implent.

And so, the battle began. The Roman army and Scipio's army clashed on the African field. The noise, clashing, and sound of weapons filled the air.

Caesar, in fronte aciei, milites suos adhortatur. "Pro Roma et gloria!" clamat. Milites, voce imperatoris sui excitati, fortius pugnant.

Caesar, at the front of the line, encouraged his soldiers. "For Rome and glory!" he shouted. The soldiers, inspired by their commander's voice, fought more fiercely.

Scipio, in altera parte, milites suos ad virtutem hortatur. "Nolite cedere! Fortiter pugnate!" clamat.

Scipio, on the other side, urged his soldiers to bravery. "Do not give up! Fight bravely!" he shouted.

Equites Romanorum in hostes impetum faciunt. Pedites fortiter pugnant, gladiis et scutis utentes. Sagittarii sagittas mittunt, hostes vulnerantes.

The Roman cavalry charged into the enemy. The infantry fought bravely, using their swords and shields. The archers shot arrows, wounding the enemy.

Amid this chaos, Caesar and Scipio, the great leaders, led their soldiers to victory. The war in Africa was great and terrible, but the Romans were strong and brave.

Et in hac pugna, sub sole Africano ardente, historia Romana scripta est. Caesar, dux magnus, et Scipio, adversarius eius, in campo Africano pro gloria et imperio pugnant.

And in this battle, under the burning African sun, Roman history was written. Caesar, the great leader, and Scipio, his adversary, fought for glory and empire on the African field.

Capitulum Tertium: Pugna Committitur

In campo bellico, sub sole ardente, Caesariani fortiter pugnant. Hostium acies fortis et numerosa est, sed Romani non terrentur.

On the battlefield, under the burning sun, Caesar's men fight bravely. The enemy's line is strong and numerous, but the Romans are not afraid.

"Pro Roma!" Caesariani clamant. Hostes fortiter resistunt, et clamor magnus in campo auditur. Tumultus magnus est, et pulvis altus in aere volat.

"For Rome!" Caesar's men shout. The enemies resist fiercely, and great shouting is heard on the battlefield. There is great turmoil, and dust rises high into the air.

Scipio, dux hostium, aciem suam instigat. "Nolite cedere, pugnate!" clamat. Milites eius clamatibus respondent.

Scipio, the enemy leader, urges on his line. "Do not give up, fight!" he shouts. His soldiers respond with shouts.

Caesar, in fronte pugnans, exemplar virtutis est. Gladium suum vibrat et hostes audacter aggreditur. "Sequimini me!" imperat.

Caesar, fighting at the front, is a model of courage. He swings his sword and boldly attacks the enemy. "Follow me!" he commands.

Equites Romani, velociter equitantes, hostes circumveniunt. Hostium acies turbatur. Equorum hinnitus et strepitus armorum resonant.

The Roman cavalry, riding swiftly, surround the enemy. The enemy line is thrown into disorder. The neighing of horses and the clashing of weapons resound.

In acie, gladii et scuta fortiter colliduntur. Viri fortes utrimque pugnant. Vulnera utrimque fiunt, sanguis in terra cadit.

In the line, swords and shields clash forcefully. Brave men fight on both sides. Wounds are inflicted on both sides, and blood falls to the ground.

Caesar, videns suos milites laborare, eos animat. "Fortes estote! Non deficimus!" exclamat. Milites eius, Caesaris verbis incitati, fortius pugnant.

Caesar, seeing his soldiers struggling, encourages them. "Be strong! We do not give up!" he shouts. His soldiers, inspired by Caesar's words, fight harder.

Hostes, Romana virtute pressi, paulatim cedunt. Romanorum animi crescunt, et impetum renovant.

The enemies, overwhelmed by Roman courage, gradually retreat. The spirits of the Romans rise, and they renew their attack.

Pedites Romani, gladiis in hostes directis, impetum renovant. Equites, fugam hostium persequuntur, hostes in fugam vertunt.

The Roman infantry, with their swords aimed at the enemy, renew their assault. The cavalry pursue the fleeing enemies, turning them to flight.

Multa caedes in campo fit. Multos hostes cadere videmus. Pugna cruenta et aspera est, sed Romani non desistunt.

Great slaughter takes place on the battlefield. We see many enemies fall. The battle is bloody and harsh, but the Romans do not stop.

Caesar, in medio pugnae, victoriam praesentit. "Hodie vincemus!" clamat. Milites eius, spe victoriae pleni, fortiter pugnant.

Caesar, in the middle of the battle, senses victory. "Today we will win!" he shouts. His soldiers, full of hope for victory, fight fiercely.

Tamen, pugna adhuc incerta est. Hostes resistunt et Romani fortiter pugnant. Nemo scit quis victor erit.

However, the battle is still uncertain. The enemies resist, and the Romans fight bravely. No one knows who will be the victor.

Sagittarii, ex locis altis, sagittas in hostes mittunt. Pugna acrior et acerbior fit. Milites utrimque fortiter pugnant, et clamores magni sunt.

The archers, from high positions, shoot arrows at the enemy. The battle becomes fiercer and more intense. Soldiers on both sides fight bravely, and the shouts are loud.

Caesar, dux magnus, in fronte manet. Hostes aspiciens, milites suos ad ultimum conatum hortatur. "Nunc est tempus!" exclamat.

Caesar, the great leader, remains at the front. Looking at the enemy, he urges his soldiers to one last effort. "Now is the time!" he exclaims.

In hoc capitulo, fortitudo et virtus Romanorum in acie clara est. Caesar, dux peritus et audax, milites suos ad victoriam ducit. Pugna in Africa, sub sole ardente, historiae paginas implet.

In this chapter, the strength and courage of the Romans in battle are clear. Caesar, a skilled and bold leader, leads his soldiers to victory. The battle in Africa, under the burning sun, fills the pages of history.

Capitulum Quartum: Victoria Caesaris

Post longam et asperam pugnam, Caesar hostes fortiter premere perseverat. Milites eius, fessi sed animosi, ad victoriam contendunt.

After a long and difficult battle, Caesar continues to press the enemy fiercely. His soldiers, weary but determined, strive for victory.

Scipio, dux hostium, desperationem sentit. Videt suos milites cedere et fugam parare. "Heu! Fortuna nos deserit!" exclamat Scipio.

Scipio, the enemy leader, feels despair. He sees his soldiers retreating and preparing to flee. "Alas! Fortune abandons us!" Scipio exclaims.

Caesariani, audientes hostes cedere, magis instigant. "Prosequimini eos!" Caesar clamat. Milites, Caesaris voce incitati, hostes vehementer persequuntur.

Caesar's men, hearing the enemy retreat, press forward more eagerly. "Pursue them!" Caesar shouts. The soldiers, inspired by Caesar's voice, vigorously pursue the enemy.

Subito, hostium acies in fugam vertitur. Milites Scipionis, terrore affecti, campum relinquunt. Clamores victoriae per castra Romana resonant.

Suddenly, the enemy line turns to flight. Scipio's soldiers, struck with terror, leave the battlefield. Shouts of victory echo through the Roman camp.

"Victoria est nostra!" Caesar exclamat, gladium suum in aere tollens. Milites, victoriam capientes, gaudio exsultant. Laeti sunt, quod pugna difficilis tandem finita est.

"Victory is ours!" Caesar exclaims, raising his sword in the air. The soldiers, realizing their victory, rejoice with joy. They are happy that the difficult battle has finally ended.

In campo bellico, multa spolia capiuntur. Arma, scuta, et alia praeda a Romanis collecta sunt. Milites spolia inter se dividunt, victoriae signa.

On the battlefield, much loot is taken. Weapons, shields, and other spoils are collected by the Romans. The soldiers divide the spoils among themselves as symbols of victory.

Scipio, videns se victum esse, fugit. Cum paucis fidelibus, nocte tectus, ex campo discedit. "Iterum pugnabimus," sibi dicit.

Scipio, seeing that he is defeated, flees. With a few loyal followers, under the cover of night, he leaves the battlefield. "We will fight again," he says to himself.

Caesar, victoria potitus, in castra revertitur. Milites eum acclamant, laudibus eum celebrant. "Caesar, dux magnus et victor!" clamant.

Caesar, having gained victory, returns to camp. The soldiers cheer him, praising him with great celebration. "Caesar, great leader and victor!" they shout.

Ad castra reversus, Caesar grates diis agit. Sacrificium facit, deorum benevolentiam recognoscens. "Deis gratias ago pro victoria," dicit.

Returning to camp, Caesar gives thanks to the gods. He performs a sacrifice, acknowledging the favor of the gods. "I give thanks to the gods for the victory," he says.

In animo suo, Caesar triumphum in Roma meditatur. Imaginat se per vias urbis incedentem, populo Romano victoriam demonstrantem.

In his mind, Caesar contemplates a triumph in Rome. He imagines himself walking through the streets of the city, showing the Roman people the victory.

Nuntii ad Romam mittuntur, victoriam pronuntiantes. Nuntii per vias urbis currunt, "Victoria! Caesar vicit!" clamantes.

Messengers are sent to Rome, announcing the victory. The messengers run through the streets of the city, shouting, "Victory! Caesar has won!"

Roma, nuntios audiens, laetitia afficitur. Populus in viis celebrat, "Caesar! Caesar!" clamantes. Laetitia et gratulatio ubique sunt.

Rome, hearing the news, is filled with joy. The people celebrate in the streets, shouting, "Caesar! Caesar!" Joy and celebration are everywhere.

Caesar, Romam reversus, honores magnos accipit. Senatus eum laudat, populus eum veneratur. "Caesar, heros et victor!" dicunt omnes.

Caesar, having returned to Rome, receives great honors. The Senate praises him, and the people revere him. "Caesar, hero and victor!" everyone says.

Pax in Africa restituitur. Caesar provincias stabilire curat, leges et ordinem restituens. Africa, post bellum, tranquillitas et prosperitas redit.

Peace is restored in Africa. Caesar takes care to stabilize the provinces, restoring laws and order. After the war, tranquility and prosperity return to Africa.

Hoc capitulo, Caesar, dux Romanus, victoriam magnam reportat. Per eius ducatum, Roma gloriam et honorem accipit. Pax et securitas in provinciis Romanis restituuntur, et Caesar ut heros et imperator celebratur.

In this chapter, Caesar, the Roman leader, achieves a great victory. Through his leadership, Rome receives glory and honor. Peace and security are restored in the Roman provinces, and Caesar is celebrated as a hero and emperor.

Capitulum Quintum: Post Bellum

Bellum in Africa finitum est. Caesar, victor et dux magnus, Africae praeficitur. In terra pacata, novam vitam incipit.

The war in Africa is over. Caesar, the victor and great leader, is placed in charge of Africa. In the peaceful land, he begins a new life.

Caesar leges et ordines in provinciis Africanis statuit. "Iustitia et pax esse debent," in concilio dicit Caesar. Legati et praefecti novas leges observant.

Caesar establishes laws and order in the African provinces. "There must be justice and peace," Caesar says in the council. Governors and officials observe the new laws.

In Africa, coloniae novae Romanae constituuntur. Homines ex Italia veniunt et terram colunt. Domus et villae aedificantur, agri coluntur.

In Africa, new Roman colonies are established. People come from Italy and cultivate the land. Houses and villas are built, and the fields are farmed.

Viae magnae et latae aedificantur. Milites et servi vias struunt. Viae commercium et communicationem inter urbes augent.

Great and wide roads are built. Soldiers and slaves construct the roads. The roads increase trade and communication between cities.

Commercium inter Africam et Romam augeatur. Navibus mercibusque, divitiae ad Africam et Romam fluunt. Forum Romanum plenum est mercatoribus et negotiis.

Trade between Africa and Rome increases. With ships and goods, wealth flows to Africa and Rome. The Roman Forum is full of merchants and business.

Cultura Romana in Africa diffunditur. Theatra, balnea, et fora Romana aedificantur. Lingua Latina et mores Romani docentur.

Roman culture spreads in Africa. Roman theaters, baths, and forums are built. The Latin language and Roman customs are taught.

Pax longa in Africa manet. Homines securi et felices sunt. "Gratias Caesar," incolae dicunt. Pax et prosperitas sunt dona Caesaris.

A long peace remains in Africa. The people are safe and happy. "Thank you, Caesar," the inhabitants say. Peace and prosperity are Caesar's gifts.

In Roma, populus Romanus Caesarem laudat. "Caesar, pacis et victoriae auctor!" clamant in foro. Caesar est heros Romanorum.

In Rome, the Roman people praise Caesar. "Caesar, the author of peace and victory!" they shout in the forum. Caesar is the hero of the Romans.

Historia Caesaris et victoriae eius scribitur. Scriptor historiae, cum charta et calamo, res gestas Caesaris narrat. Libri de Caesaris rebus gestis in scholis leguntur.

The history of Caesar and his victory is written. The historian, with paper and pen, records the deeds of Caesar. Books about Caesar's accomplishments are read in schools.

Caesar, post rem gestam in Africa, Romam redit. Urbs eum magna cum laetitia excipit. "Caesar redit!" pueri in viis clamant.

Caesar, after his accomplishments in Africa, returns to Rome. The city receives him with great joy. "Caesar returns!" children shout in the streets.

Triumphus magnificus in urbe fit. Caesar, laurea coronatus, in curru triumphali stat. Equi albi currum trahunt, et populus plaudit.

A magnificent triumph is held in the city. Caesar, crowned with laurel, stands in a triumphal chariot. White horses pull the chariot, and the people applaud.

Caesar in senatu loquitur. "Pax et securitas in provinciis nostris sunt," dicit. Senatores eum audiunt et consiliis eius assentiunt.

Caesar speaks in the Senate. "Peace and security are in our provinces," he says. The senators listen to him and agree with his plans.

Caesar nova consilia pro imperio Romano narrat. "Novas terras explorabimus, novas vias aedificabimus," promittit. Senatores et populus consiliis eius favent.

Caesar announces new plans for the Roman Empire. "We will explore new lands, and we will build new roads," he promises. The senators and the people support his plans.

Populus Romanus Caesaris victorias et pacem celebrat. Festa et ludos in urbe fiunt. "Vivat Caesar!" omnes clamant.

The Roman people celebrate Caesar's victories and peace. Festivals and games are held in the city. "Long live Caesar!" everyone shouts.

Caesar non solum magnus dux est, sed etiam fama vivens efficitur. Res eius gestae in historia Romana manebunt. Caesar, dux et imperator, in memoria populi Romani semper erit.

Caesar is not only a great leader but also becomes a living legend. His deeds will remain in Roman history. Caesar, leader and emperor, will always be in the memory of the Roman people.

In hoc capitulo, Caesar, post victoriam in Africa, pacem et prosperitatem in provincias Romanas afferit. Cultura Romana floruit, et Caesar, ut dux et pacis auctor, in historia Romana immortalis fit.

In this chapter, Caesar, after his victory in Africa, brings peace and prosperity to the Roman provinces. Roman culture flourishes, and Caesar, as a leader and bringer of peace, becomes immortal in Roman history.

Capitulum Sextum: Legati Africani

Legati Africani, ornatu et vestitu splendido, Romam veniunt. Per vias urbis incedunt, populus Romanus eos spectat.

The African envoys, in splendid attire and clothing, come to Rome. They walk through the streets of the city, and the Roman people watch them.

In foro Romano, Caesar, in toga praetexta, eos accipit. "Salvete, legati Africani," dicit Caesar. Legati, "Salve, Caesar," respondent.

In the Roman Forum, Caesar, wearing a toga with a purple border, receives them. "Greetings, African envoys," says Caesar. The envoys respond, "Greetings, Caesar."

In curia, foedera inter Romanos et Africanos fiunt. Chartae et calami adhibentur, et legati manibus foedera signant. "Pax inter nos sit," dicit Caesar.

In the Senate house, treaties between the Romans and Africans are made. Papers and pens are used, and the envoys sign the treaties with their hands. "Let there be peace between us," says Caesar.

Africa, olim hostilis, nunc Romae amica est. Commercia inter terras incipiunt. Navis onerariae in portu Romano apponuntur, mercibus Africani plenae.

Africa, once hostile, is now a friend to Rome. Trade between the lands begins. Merchant ships dock at the Roman port, filled with African goods.

Culturae Romana et Africana inter se miscentur. Homines Romani Africanos mores discunt, et vice versa. Utriusque terrae artes et scientiae communicantur.

Roman and African cultures mix with each other. Roman people learn African customs, and vice versa. The arts and sciences of both lands are shared.

In scholis Romanis, studia Africana crescunt. Discipuli de Africa discunt, de eius terra, animalibus, et populo. Libri et chartae de Africa in bibliothecis reperiuntur.

In Roman schools, studies about Africa grow. Students learn about Africa, its land, animals, and people. Books and papers about Africa are found in libraries.

In theatris Romanis, ars Africana celebratur. Cantores et saltatores Africani spectacula praebebunt. Populus Romanus eorum artibus delectatur.

In Roman theaters, African art is celebrated. African singers and dancers will perform shows. The Roman people delight in their arts.

Inter Romanos et Africanos, pax et amicitia confirmantur. "Pax nobis bonum est," dicit Caesar in foro publico. Populus plaudit et acclamat.

Between the Romans and Africans, peace and friendship are strengthened. "Peace is good for us," says Caesar in the public forum. The people applaud and cheer.

Caesar pro eius sapientia et virtute laudes accipit. "Caesar, dux magnus et sapiens!" clamat populus. Senatus etiam gratias ei agit pro pacis operibus.

Caesar receives praise for his wisdom and virtue. "Caesar, a great and wise leader!" the people shout. The Senate also thanks him for his work in securing peace.

In Africa, populus Africanus prosperat. Agricolae terram colunt, mercatores negotiantur, et artifices artes suas exercent. Vita in Africa melior fit.

In Africa, the African people prosper. Farmers cultivate the land, merchants trade, and craftsmen practice their arts. Life in Africa becomes better.

Roma et Africa, manu in manu, florent. Commercia, cultura, et scientia inter terras augent. "Roma et Africa, amici aeterni," dicit Caesar.

Rome and Africa, hand in hand, flourish. Trade, culture, and knowledge between the lands increase. "Rome and Africa, eternal friends," says Caesar.

Historiae novae de pace et amicitia inter Romanos et Africanos scribuntur. Scriptor in tablino sedet, historiam novam narrans. "Haec est historia pacis et amicitiae," scribit.

New histories about peace and friendship between the Romans and Africans are written. A writer sits in his study, telling the new story. "This is the history of peace and friendship," he writes.

Caesar et Africa, in historiam Romanam intrant. Res gestae Caesaris et pacis cum Africanis in annalibus Romanorum manebunt. "Caesar et Africa, exempla pacis," in libris leguntur.

Caesar and Africa enter Roman history. Caesar's deeds and the peace with the Africans will remain in the Roman records. "Caesar and Africa, examples of peace," are read in books.

Hoc capitulo, legati Africani ad Romam veniunt et foedera cum Romanis faciunt. Pax et amicitia inter duas terras confirmantur. Caesar pro eius operibus laudatur, et Roma et Africa in novam aetatem pacis et prosperitatis intrant.

In this chapter, African envoys come to Rome and make treaties with the Romans. Peace and friendship between the two lands are confirmed. Caesar is praised for his work, and Rome and Africa enter a new age of peace and prosperity.

Capitulum Septimum: Caesaris Sapientia

Caesar, imperator Romanus, consiliis sapientibus utitur. In curia Romana, cum senatoribus loquitur. "Leges iustas et aequas introducamus," dicit Caesar.

Caesar, the Roman emperor, uses wise plans. In the Roman Senate, he speaks with the senators. "Let us introduce just and fair laws," says Caesar.

Leges et iura in imperio Romano introducit. "Iura omnibus civibus dabuntur," promittit. Populus Romanus eius leges laudat.

He introduces laws and rights into the Roman Empire. "Rights will be given to all citizens," he promises. The Roman people praise his laws.

Caesar exemplar imperatoris fit. In foro, populus eum spectat et admiratur. "Caesar, dux magnus!" clamant.

Caesar becomes a model of leadership. In the forum, the people watch and admire him. "Caesar, great leader!" they shout.

In castris, doctrina militari utitur. Milites exercet et disciplinam docet. "Disciplina est fortitudo," dicit Caesar militibus.

In the camps, he uses military doctrine. He trains the soldiers and teaches discipline. "Discipline is strength," says Caesar to the soldiers.

Exercitus Romanus, Caesaris ductu, fortior fit. Milites in campis exercitantur, gladiis et scutis. "Fortes estote!" centurio clamat.

The Roman army, under Caesar's leadership, becomes stronger. The soldiers train in the fields, with swords and shields. "Be strong!" the centurion shouts.

Disciplina in exercitu Romano viget. Milites ordines sequuntur et imperia audiunt. "Disciplina victoriam parit," dicit Caesar.

Discipline thrives in the Roman army. The soldiers follow orders and listen to commands. "Discipline brings victory," says Caesar.

Caesar, dux amatus ab omnibus, in campis cum militibus ambulat. Milites eum salutant et honorant. "Salve, Caesar!" dicunt.

Caesar, a leader loved by all, walks in the fields with the soldiers. The soldiers greet and honor him. "Hail, Caesar!" they say.

Ars belli a Caesare perficitur. In tablino, strategias bellorum excogitat. "Strategia est clavis victoriae," cogitat Caesar.

The art of war is perfected by Caesar. In his study, he devises battle strategies. "Strategy is the key to victory," Caesar thinks.

Strategiae novae a Caesare excogitantur. In consiliis bellis, cum legatis loquitur. "Hoc modo vincemus," demonstrat in mappa.

New strategies are devised by Caesar. In war councils, he speaks with his commanders. "We will win this way," he shows on a map.

Historia militaris Romana augetur. Per victorias Caesaris, Roma potentior fit. In foro, historiae Caesaris narratur. "Magnae sunt victoriae Caesaris!" exclamant.

Roman military history grows. Through Caesar's victories, Rome becomes more powerful. In the forum, Caesar's stories are told. "Great are Caesar's victories!" they exclaim.

Caesar de bellis et victoriis scribit. In tablino sedens, commentarios de bellis Gallicis et civilibus componit. "Haec est vera historia," scribit Caesar.

Caesar writes about wars and victories. Sitting in his study, he composes commentaries on the Gallic and civil wars. "This is true history," Caesar writes.

Libri Caesaris in scholis Romanis studiis sunt. Discipuli in scholis legunt et discunt. "Caesar, magister et dux," dicit magister.

Caesar's books are studied in Roman schools. Students read and learn in the schools. "Caesar, teacher and leader," says the teacher.

Romani sapientiam Caesaris laudant. In foro, de eius consiliis et legibus loquuntur. "Caesar est sapiens et prudens," dicunt.

The Romans praise Caesar's wisdom. In the forum, they talk about his plans and laws. "Caesar is wise and prudent," they say.

Imperium Romanum sub Caesare expanditur. Novae terrae et provinciae ad imperium adduntur. "Imperium nostrum crescet," dicit Caesar in senatu.

The Roman Empire expands under Caesar. New lands and provinces are added to the empire. "Our empire will grow," says Caesar in the Senate.

Caesar, pro suis rebus gestis et sapientia, aeternum in memoria Romanorum manebit. In foro, statua Caesaris stat. "Caesar, semper memorabimus te," dicunt.

Caesar, for his accomplishments and wisdom, will remain forever in the memory of the Romans. In the forum, a statue of Caesar stands. "Caesar, we will always remember you," they say.

Hoc capitulo, Caesar, pro sua sapientia, imperium Romanum reformavit et fortificavit. Leges, disciplina militaris, et ars belli perficiuntur. Historia militaris Romana crescit, et Caesar ut dux sapientissimus et immortalis celebratur.

In this chapter, Caesar, through his wisdom, reformed and strengthened the Roman Empire. Laws, military discipline, and the art of war are perfected. Roman military history grows, and Caesar is celebrated as a most wise and immortal leader.

Capitulum Octavum: Caesaris Gloria

Julius Caesar, imperator Romanus, multas terras vincit. In Gallia, in Britannia, et in civitatibus longinquis, eius victoriae magnae sunt.

Julius Caesar, the Roman commander, conquers many lands. In Gaul, in Britain, and in distant cities, his victories are great.

Imperium Romanum sub eius ducatu amplificatur. Provincias novas imperio addit. "Imperium nostrum magnum et fortum erit," dicit Caesar.

The Roman Empire is expanded under his leadership. He adds new provinces to the empire. "Our empire will be great and strong," says Caesar.

Gloria Romae sub Caesare crescit. In foro, populus de eius victoriis loquitur. "Roma invicta est!" clamant.

Rome's glory grows under Caesar. In the forum, the people talk about his victories. "Rome is undefeated!" they shout.

Caesar exemplar virtutis et fortitudinis est. In curia, senatores eum laudant. "Caesar, virtute et sapientia praeclarus est," dicunt.

Caesar is an example of virtue and strength. In the Senate, the senators praise him. "Caesar is distinguished by virtue and wisdom," they say.

Gentes omnes Caesaris famam admirantur. Ab Hispania ad Aegyptum, eius nomen notum est. "Caesar, dux et imperator magnus!" gentes dicunt.

All nations admire Caesar's fame. From Spain to Egypt, his name is known. "Caesar, a great leader and commander!" the nations say.

Nomen Caesaris per saecula manet. In annalibus et historiis, eius gesta narratur. "Caesar, in aeternum memorabimus te," scribunt historici.

Caesar's name endures through the ages. In records and histories, his deeds are told. "Caesar, we will remember you forever," historians write.

Monumenta et statuae in honorem Caesaris aedificantur. In foro Romano, statua aurea Caesaris stat. Populus ad statuam venit et eum honorat.

Monuments and statues are built in Caesar's honor. In the Roman Forum, a golden statue of Caesar stands. The people come to the statue and honor him.

Festi et celebrationes in eius honorem fiunt. In urbe, ludis et spectaculis, Caesar celebratur. "Dies Caesaris!" populus in festis clamat.

Festivals and celebrations are held in his honor. In the city, through games and shows, Caesar is celebrated. "Caesar's Day!" the people shout at the festivals.

Poetae et scriptores carmina et poesis de Caesaris rebus gestis scribunt. In theatris, carmina eius audita sunt. "Caesar, heros et victor," poetae cantant.

Poets and writers compose songs and poetry about Caesar's achievements. In the theaters, his songs are heard. "Caesar, hero and victor," the poets sing.

Imagines Caesaris ubique sunt. In monetis, in statuis, et in picturis, eius imago videtur. "Hic est Caesar," dicunt homines, imagines spectantes.

Images of Caesar are everywhere. On coins, in statues, and in paintings, his likeness is seen. "This is Caesar," people say, looking at the images.

Caesar in historia Romana manet. Scriptor in tablino sedet et de Caesaris victoriis scribit. "Haec est historia Caesaris," narrat.

Caesar remains in Roman history. A writer sits in his study and writes about Caesar's victories. "This is the history of Caesar," he tells.

Discipuli in scholis Romanis historiam Caesaris discunt. Magister eos de bellis Gallicis et civilibus docet. "Discite de Caesaris virtute," inquit magister.

Students in Roman schools learn Caesar's history. The teacher teaches them about the Gallic and civil wars. "Learn about Caesar's virtue," the teacher says.

Opera Caesaris, sicut Commentarii de Bello Gallico, in scholis leguntur. Discipuli librum legunt et de eius rebus gestis discunt. "Caesar, magister militum," dicunt.

Caesar's works, such as the *Commentaries on the Gallic War*, are read in schools. The students read the book and learn about his achievements. "Caesar, master of soldiers," they say.

Memoria Caesaris aeterna est. In templo, sacerdotes sacrificia in eius memoriam faciunt. "Caesar, semper in corde nostro," dicunt sacerdotes.

Caesar's memory is eternal. In the temple, priests make sacrifices in his memory. "Caesar, always in our hearts," the priests say.

Caesar, vir magnus et imperator fortis, in Roma et in mundo semper celebratur. Eius vita, eius gesta, eius sapientia in historia Romana et mundi semper manebunt.

Caesar, a great man and strong commander, is always celebrated in Rome and in the world. His life, his deeds, and his wisdom will always remain in Roman and world history.

In hoc capitulo, gloria Caesaris et eius impactus in historiam Romanam et mundi illustrantur. Eius virtus, eius victoriae, et eius sapientia per saecula celebrantur, et memoria eius aeterna est.

In this chapter, Caesar's glory and his impact on Roman and world history are illustrated. His virtue, his victories, and his wisdom are celebrated through the ages, and his memory is eternal.

Caesar et Cleopatra: Amor et Imperium

Capitulum Primum: Caesar in Aegypto

Gaius Iulius Caesar, dux Romanorum, in Aegyptum venit. Alexandriam, magnam urbem, intrat. Sol altus est et caelum serenum. Cleopatra, regina Aegypti, expectat.

Gaius Julius Caesar, leader of the Romans, comes to Egypt. He enters Alexandria, the great city. The sun is high, and the sky is clear. Cleopatra, queen of Egypt, waits.

Cleopatra: "Salve, magne Caesar. Auxilium tuum mihi opus est."

Cleopatra: "Greetings, great Caesar. I need your help."

Caesar: "What do you need, queen?"

Cleopatra: "Frater meus me expellere vult. Regnum nostrum in periculo est."

Cleopatra: "My brother wants to expel me. Our kingdom is in danger."

Caesar: "Pax Romana etiam in Aegypto esse potest. Tibi auxiliabor."

Caesar: "The Roman peace can also be in Egypt. I will help you."

Cleopatra: "Gratias tibi ago, Caesar."

Cleopatra: "Thank you, Caesar."

Romani, cum Caesare, in Aegypto diutius manent. Cleopatra et Ptolemaeus, frater eius, de regno contendunt. Discordia magna erat. Ptolemaeus, iuvenis et iratus, Caesarem non audit.

The Romans, with Caesar, stay longer in Egypt. Cleopatra and Ptolemy, her brother, fight over the kingdom. There was great discord. Ptolemy, young and angry, does not listen to Caesar.

Caesar: "Cur frater et soror non in pace regnare possunt?"

Caesar: "Why can't brother and sister rule in peace?"

Ptolemaeus: "Regnum meum est! Sola regnabo!"

Ptolemy: "The kingdom is mine! I will rule alone!"

Caesar: "Non sine iure! Cleopatra iure regina est."

Caesar: "Not without justice! Cleopatra is queen by right."

Ptolemaeus, iratus, milites convocat. Caesar etiam suos milites parat. Bellum parare incipiunt. Alexandriae, urbs pulchra, nunc locus belli est. Romani urbem obsident. Caesar dicit, "Urbs nostra est!"

Ptolemy, angry, calls his soldiers. Caesar also prepares his soldiers. They begin to prepare for war. Alexandria, the beautiful city, is now the place of battle. The Romans besiege the city. Caesar says, "The city is ours!"

Cleopatra, in palatio suo, sollicita est. Romam cogitat. Romani fortes sunt, sed Aegyptii multi. Caesar autem confidit.

Cleopatra, in her palace, is worried. She thinks of Rome. The Romans are strong, but the Egyptians are many. Yet Caesar is confident.

Cleopatra: "Caesar, mea spes est in te."

Cleopatra: "Caesar, my hope is in you."

Caesar: "Noli timere, Cleopatra. Victoria nostra erit."

Caesar: "Do not fear, Cleopatra. The victory will be ours."

Bellum incipit. Clamor magnus est. Romani et Aegyptii pugnant. Gladii fulgent. Sagittae volant. Caesar imperat, "State fortes, milites!"

The war begins. There is a great clamor. The Romans and Egyptians fight. Swords flash. Arrows fly. Caesar commands, "Stand strong, soldiers!"

Nox venit. Caesar et Cleopatra in castris Romanorum loquuntur. Caesar dicit, "Nocte, consilia meliora veniunt."

Night falls. Caesar and Cleopatra talk in the Roman camp. Caesar says, "At night, better plans come."

Cleopatra: "Meum cor est tecum, Caesar. Pro Aegypto, pro Roma pugnabimus."

Cleopatra: "My heart is with you, Caesar. We will fight for Egypt, for Rome."

Capitulum Secundum: Bellum Alexandrinum

Romani et Aegyptii acriter pugnant. In viis Alexandrinae, clamores audiri possunt. Caesar, cum audacia, partes urbis fortiter occupat.

The Romans and Egyptians fight fiercely. In the streets of Alexandria, shouts can be heard. Caesar, with courage, boldly takes control of parts of the city.

Caesar: "Milites, ad portum procedite! Naves hostium capite!"

Caesar: "Soldiers, advance to the port! Capture the enemy ships!"

Navalia proelia in magno Alexandri portu sunt. Romani naves Aegyptias igni incendunt. Flammae altae in caelum surgunt. Caesar, in prora navis, Romanos ad victoriam ducit.

Naval battles take place in the great port of Alexandria. The Romans set the Egyptian ships on fire. Flames rise high into the sky. Caesar, on the bow of a ship, leads the Romans to victory.

Cleopatra, a palatio spectans, timet.

Cleopatra, watching from the palace, is afraid.

Cleopatra: "O dii, salvum Caesarem facite!"

Cleopatra: "Oh gods, keep Caesar safe!"

Caesar, hostium circumdatus, in magno periculo est. Sed non terretur. Militibus magna voce imperat.

Caesar, surrounded by enemies, is in great danger. But he is not afraid. He gives orders to his soldiers in a loud voice.

Caesar: "Nolite timere! Fortiter pugnate!"

Caesar: "Do not fear! Fight bravely!"

Ptolemaeus, videns Romanos valere, fugere conatur. Sed Romani sunt fortes et celeres. Ptolemaeus captus est. Catenis in manibus, trahitur.

Ptolemy, seeing the Romans gaining strength, tries to flee. But the Romans are strong and swift. Ptolemy is captured. He is dragged in chains, with his hands bound.

Caesar, captivum Ptolemaeum videns, dicit: "Aegyptus nunc pacem habebit."

Caesar, seeing the captive Ptolemy, says: "Egypt will now have peace."

Cleopatra, gaudio plena, Caesarem laudat.

Cleopatra, full of joy, praises Caesar.

Cleopatra: "Caesar, sine te non vinceremus!"

Cleopatra: "Caesar, without you, we would not have won!"

Pax tandem in Aegypto restituitur. Caesar, reginae Cleopatrae favens, regnum eius confirmat.

Peace is finally restored in Egypt. Caesar, favoring Queen Cleopatra, confirms her reign.

Caesar: "Cleopatra, tu regina Aegypti eris. Populus Romanus te adiuvabit."

Caesar: "Cleopatra, you will be the queen of Egypt. The Roman people will support you."

Romani et Aegyptii, victoria celebrata, laetantur. Festa per totam urbem fiunt. Cleopatra et Caesar, una cum populo, diem festum agunt.

The Romans and Egyptians, celebrating the victory, rejoice. Festivals are held throughout the city. Cleopatra and Caesar, together with the people, celebrate the festive day.

Capitulum Tertium: Amor et Politica

Caesar et Cleopatra amorem inter se habent. Cleopatra Caesarem in regiam suam invitat.

Caesar and Cleopatra share love for one another. Cleopatra invites Caesar to her palace.

Cleopatra: "Veni, Caesar, et Aegypti gloriam vide."

Cleopatra: "Come, Caesar, and see the glory of Egypt."

Caesar, cum Cleopatra ambulans, de magnis rebus cogitat.

Caesar, walking with Cleopatra, thinks of great matters.

Caesar: "Roma et Aegyptus simul potentes esse possunt."

Caesar: "Rome and Egypt together can be powerful."

Cleopatra multa de Aegypto Caesari docet. Caesar historiam bellorum narrat.

Cleopatra teaches Caesar much about Egypt. Caesar tells the story of wars.

Caesar: "Bella multa vidi. Nunc pacem in Aegypto volo."

Caesar: "I have seen many wars. Now I want peace in Egypt."

Cleopatra, amata et audita, Caesari filium parit. Puer Caesarion appellatur.

Cleopatra, loved and heard, bears a son for Caesar. The boy is named Caesarion.

Romani de Caesare et Cleopatra multa fabulantur. Nonnulli laudant, alii sunt critici.

The Romans gossip much about Caesar and Cleopatra. Some praise them, others criticize.

Caesar et Cleopatra in Nilo navigant. Flumen est pulchrum et tranquillum.

Caesar and Cleopatra sail on the Nile. The river is beautiful and calm.

Cleopatra: "Consilia tua magna sunt. Te adiuvabo."

Cleopatra: "Your plans are great. I will help you."

Caesar: "Cum tuo auxilio, Aegyptus florebit."

Caesar: "With your help, Egypt will flourish."

Sed Caesar Romam redire debet. Cleopatra est tristis, Caesar eam consolatur.

But Caesar must return to Rome. Cleopatra is sad, and Caesar comforts her.

Caesar: "Romam redeo, sed in corde meo semper eris. Promitto, reveniam."

Caesar: "I am returning to Rome, but you will always be in my heart. I promise, I will return."

Cleopatra lacrimat. Caesar in navigium ascendit et ad Romam navigat.

Cleopatra weeps. Caesar boards the ship and sails to Rome.

Capitulum Quartum: Caesar in Roma

Caesar post multa bella Romam redit. Urbs eum laeta salutat.

Caesar returns to Rome after many wars. The city happily greets him.

Romani: "Caesar, triumphum tuum celebramus!"

The Romans: "Caesar, we celebrate your triumph!"

Caesar, in curru, per vias urbis vehitur. De Cleopatra et Aegypto saepe cogitat.

Caesar, in a chariot, is carried through the streets of the city. He often thinks of Cleopatra and Egypt.

In senatu Romae, de magnis rebus loquuntur.

In the Roman Senate, they talk about important matters.

Senator: "De Caesare et regina Aegyptia, Cleopatra, quid dicimus?"

Senator: "What do we say about Caesar and Cleopatra, the queen of Egypt?"

Caesar in foro Romano consul proclamatur. Plausus magnus auditur.

Caesar is proclaimed consul in the Roman Forum. Loud applause is heard.

Caesar: "Leges novas pro populo Romano faciam."

Caesar: "I will make new laws for the Roman people."

Cleopatra in Aegypto de Roma cogitat et venire Romam in animo habet.

Cleopatra in Egypt thinks about Rome and has plans to come to Rome.

Romani: "Audistisne de Cleopatra? Rumores circumeunt!"

Romans: "Have you heard about Cleopatra? Rumors are spreading!"

Caesar in senatu laudatus est ob virtutes eius.

Caesar is praised in the Senate for his virtues.

Senator: "Caesar, pro pace et legibus novis gratias agimus."

Senator: "Caesar, we thank you for peace and new laws."

Caesar de pace in senatu disserit.

Caesar speaks about peace in the Senate.

Caesar: "Pax nobis maximi momenti est."

Caesar: "Peace is of the greatest importance to us."

Cleopatra, sollicita, epistulam longam ad Caesarem mittit.

Cleopatra, worried, sends a long letter to Caesar.

Cleopatra: "Caesar, te desidero. De nobis quid futurum est?"

Cleopatra: "Caesar, I miss you. What will become of us?"

Caesar epistulam accipit et statim respondet.

Caesar receives the letter and immediately responds.

Caesar: "Cleopatra, auxilium tibi semper dabo. Ne time."

Caesar: "Cleopatra, I will always help you. Do not fear."

Cleopatra, verba Caesaris legens, paulo melius se sentit.

Cleopatra, reading Caesar's words, feels a little better.

Cleopatra: "Spero nos iterum convenire."

Cleopatra: "I hope we will meet again."

Caesar et Cleopatra epistulas saepe mittunt, amor et politica semper in verbis latent.

Caesar and Cleopatra often exchange letters, with love and politics always hidden in their words.

Capitulum Quintum: Idus Martiae

Caesar in Roma potentiam maximam habet et dictator perpetuus nominatur. Sed non omnes laeti sunt.

Caesar holds the greatest power in Rome and is named dictator for life. But not everyone is happy.

Romanus: "Dictator perpetuus? Quid de republica?"

A Roman: "Dictator for life? What about the republic?"

Romani inter se de Caesare loquuntur et solliciti sunt de futura libertate.

The Romans talk among themselves about Caesar and are worried about the future of their freedom.

Cleopatra in Aegypto est et de Caesare, amato suo, semper cogitat.

Cleopatra is in Egypt and always thinks about Caesar, her beloved.

Cleopatra: "Quid agit meus Caesar in Roma?"

Cleopatra: "What is my Caesar doing in Rome?"

Coniurationes in senatu fiunt. Senatores occulte contra Caesarem consilia capiunt.

Conspiracies form in the Senate. Senators secretly plot against Caesar.

Senator: "Caesar nimis potens est. Agere debemus!"

Senator: "Caesar is too powerful. We must act!"

Idus Martiae, dies fatalis, appropinquant. Omnia in urbe tensa sunt.

The Ides of March, the fateful day, approaches. Everything in the city is tense.

Amicus Caesaris: "Caesar, cave Idus Martiae! Periculum est!"

A friend of Caesar: "Caesar, beware the Ides of March! There is danger!"

Caesar, vir fortis, non timet. "Fortuna fortibus favet," dicit.

Caesar, a brave man, is not afraid. "Fortune favors the bold," he says.

Nocte ante Idus, Cleopatra somnium terribile habet. Caesar sanguine cecidit.

On the night before the Ides, Cleopatra has a terrible dream. Caesar fell, covered in blood.

Cleopatra: "Omina mala sentio!"

Cleopatra: "I feel bad omens!"

Die Idus Martiae, Caesar ad curiam venit. Coniurati cum pugionibus celatis exspectant.

On the Ides of March, Caesar comes to the Senate. The conspirators wait with hidden daggers.

Coniuratus: "Nunc agendum est. Pro libertate!"

A conspirator: "Now is the time to act. For freedom!"

Caesar, curiam ingressus, salutatur. Subito, coniurati surgunt et eum pugionibus petunt.

Caesar, having entered the Senate, is greeted. Suddenly, the conspirators rise and attack him with daggers.

Caesar: "Et tu, Brute?"

Caesar: "And you, Brutus?"

Nuntius celeriter per urbes currit. Cleopatra de morte Caesaris audit.

A messenger quickly runs through the cities. Cleopatra hears of Caesar's death.

Nuntius: "Caesar occisus est!"

Messenger: "Caesar has been killed!"

Roma in chaos versatur. Homines in viis currunt et clamant.

Rome is thrown into chaos. People run and shout in the streets.

Cleopatra, audito nuntio, dolore conficitur. Romam venire desiderat, sed non potest.

Cleopatra, hearing the news, is overwhelmed with grief. She wishes to go to Rome, but she cannot.

Cleopatra: "Roma ardet et amor meus extinctus est!"

Cleopatra: "Rome burns, and my love is extinguished!"

Caesarion, puer parvus, nescit patrem iam non esse.

Caesarion, the young boy, does not know that his father is no longer alive.

Cleopatra, sola et maerens, ad statuam Caesaris loquitur.

Cleopatra, alone and grieving, speaks to Caesar's statue.

Cleopatra: "Amor meus, numquam te obliviscar. Semper in corde meo manebis."

Cleopatra: "My love, I will never forget you. You will always remain in my heart."

Capitulum Sextum: Cleopatra et Antonius

Marcus Antonius, amicus Caesaris, nunc Romae potens est. Cleopatra eum in Aegypto videre cupit.

Mark Antony, a friend of Caesar, is now powerful in Rome. Cleopatra wishes to see him in Egypt.

Cleopatra: "Antonium convenire cupio."

Cleopatra: "I wish to meet Antony."

Antonius, Cleopatrae desiderium audiens, in Aegyptum venit.

Antony, hearing Cleopatra's desire, comes to Egypt.

Antonius: "Cleopatra, venio ut te videam."

Antony: "Cleopatra, I come to see you."

Cleopatra et Antonius in palatio reginae conveniunt. Foedus inter se faciunt.

Cleopatra and Antony meet in the queen's palace. They make an alliance with each other.

Antonius: "Cleopatra, te amo et tecum foedus facio."

Antony: "Cleopatra, I love you, and I make an alliance with you."

Cleopatra, regina sapientissima, de Aegypto et de Roma cogitat.

Cleopatra, the very wise queen, thinks about Egypt and Rome.

Cleopatra: "Aegyptus et Roma simul potentes esse possunt."

Cleopatra: "Egypt and Rome together can be powerful."

Antonius Cleopatram reginam appellat et eam magnifice honorat.

Antony calls Cleopatra a queen and honors her magnificently.

Romani in foro de Antonio et Cleopatra loquuntur.

The Romans talk in the forum about Antony and Cleopatra.

Romanus: "Audistisne de Antonio et Cleopatra?"

A Roman: "Have you heard about Antony and Cleopatra?"

Cleopatra Antonio in rebus difficilibus adiuvat. Antonius Romam redit.

Cleopatra helps Antony in difficult matters. Antony returns to Rome.

Cleopatra: "Antonium exspecto et spero eum mox rediturum."

Cleopatra: "I wait for Antony and hope he will return soon."

Antonius in Roma bellum parat. Id necessarium est. Cleopatra naves et opes Antonio dat.

Antony prepares for war in Rome. It is necessary. Cleopatra gives Antony ships and resources.

Cleopatra: "Antonio auxilium meum do."

Cleopatra: "I give my help to Antony."

Bellum civile incipit. Tempus difficile est. Cleopatra et Antonius socii sunt.

The civil war begins. It is a difficult time. Cleopatra and Antony are allies.

Antonius: "Cleopatra, tecum sumus in hoc bello."

Antony: "Cleopatra, we are with you in this war."

Capitulum Septimum: Bellum Actiacum

Antonius et Cleopatra magnam classem parant. Naves longas et veloces aedificant.

Antony and Cleopatra prepare a great fleet. They build long and fast ships.

Cleopatra: "Classis nostra parata est. Victoria nostra erit!"

Cleopatra: "Our fleet is ready. Victory will be ours!"

Augustus, adversarius Antonii, contra eum movet. Mox, apud Actium, proelium navale fit.

Augustus, Antony's rival, moves against him. Soon, a naval battle takes place at Actium.

Nuntius: "Proelium Actiacum incipit!"

Messenger: "The Battle of Actium begins!"

In proelio, Antonius et Cleopatra fortiter pugnant. Naves Romanas petunt.

In the battle, Antony and Cleopatra fight bravely. They attack the Roman ships.

Cleopatra: "Antoni, pugna! Non desistas!"

Cleopatra: "Antony, fight! Do not give up!"

Sed Augustus, dux Romanus, fortis et astutus est. Proelium durum est.

But Augustus, the Roman leader, is strong and cunning. The battle is hard.

Augustus: "Romani, vincite! Hoc proelium nostrum est!"

Augustus: "Romans, win! This battle is ours!"

Tandem, Augustus proelium vincit. Antonius et Cleopatra fugere cogitant.

At last, Augustus wins the battle. Antony and Cleopatra think about fleeing.

Antonius: "Cleopatra, fugere debemus. Hic manere periculosum est."

Antony: "Cleopatra, we must flee. It is dangerous to stay here."

Fugientes, Aegyptum petunt. Romani eos sequuntur. Aegyptus in periculo est.

Fleeing, they head to Egypt. The Romans follow them. Egypt is in danger.

Antonius, desperatus, de vita sua desperat. Victoria Romana imminet.

Antony, in despair, loses hope for his life. Roman victory is imminent.

Cleopatra: "Antoni, ne desperes! Adhuc sperare debemus."

Cleopatra: "Antony, do not despair! We must still have hope."

Augustus, cum exercitu suo, Alexandriam venit. Urbs in periculo est.

Augustus arrives in Alexandria with his army. The city is in danger.

Cleopatra Augustum orat: "Parce nobis! Parce Aegypto!"

Cleopatra begs Augustus: "Spare us! Spare Egypt!"

Antonius, amore plenus, se interficit. Vult Cleopatrae parcere.

Antony, full of love, takes his own life. He wants to spare Cleopatra.

Antonius: "Vale, Cleopatra. Amor meus semper tuus erit."

Antony: "Farewell, Cleopatra. My love will always be yours."

Cleopatra, vidua et regina, de Aegypto cogitat. Roma potens est.

Cleopatra, widow and queen, thinks about Egypt. Rome is powerful.

Cleopatra: "Non Romae serviam. Libera nata sum, libera moriar!"

Cleopatra: "I will not serve Rome. I was born free, and I will die free!"

Cleopatra, regina nobilis, mortem suam eligit. Aegyptus nunc Romanae provinciae fit.

Cleopatra, the noble queen, chooses her own death. Egypt now becomes a Roman province.

Nuntius: "Aegyptus nunc est sub dominio Romano!"

Messenger: "Egypt is now under Roman rule!"

Capitulum Octavum: Hereditas

Caesarion, filius Caesaris et Cleopatrae, ultimus rex Aegypti manet. Sed tempora difficilia sunt.

Caesarion, the son of Caesar and Cleopatra, remains the last king of Egypt. But these are difficult times.

Romanus: "Aegyptus nunc nostra est. Imperium Romanum regnat."

A Roman: "Egypt is now ours. The Roman Empire rules."

Memoria Cleopatrae in historia manet. Cleopatra non obliviscitur.

The memory of Cleopatra remains in history. Cleopatra is not forgotten.

Historicus: "Cleopatra, regina Aegypti, semper in historiis manebit."

Historian: "Cleopatra, queen of Egypt, will always remain in history."

Roma divitias magnas ex Aegypto capit. Aegyptus opulentia sua carere cogitur.

Rome takes great riches from Egypt. Egypt is forced to part with its wealth.

Romanus: "Vide, quam divites sumus ob Aegyptum!"

A Roman: "Look how rich we are because of Egypt!"

Dolor Romanorum: Caesarion occiditur. Nullus de regali familia superest.

The sorrow of the Romans: Caesarion is killed. No one from the royal family remains.

Romanus: "Caesarion, rex iuvenis, a nobis occisus est."

A Roman: "Caesarion, the young king, was killed by us."

Cultus Aegypti ad Romam venit. Romani deorum Aegyptiorum ritus discunt.

Egyptian culture comes to Rome. The Romans learn the rituals of the Egyptian gods.

Romanus: "Dei Aegypti nobis novi et mirabiles sunt."

A Roman: "The gods of Egypt are new and marvelous to us."

In arte, Cleopatra et Caesar semper vivunt. Picturae et statuae eorum fiunt.

In art, Cleopatra and Caesar live on forever. Paintings and statues of them are made.

Pictor: "Cleopatram et Caesarem pingimus, ut semper meminerimus."

Painter: "We paint Cleopatra and Caesar so we may always remember them."

Scriptores fabulas multas de Cleopatra scribunt. Cleopatra in libris vivit.

Writers create many stories about Cleopatra. Cleopatra lives in books.

Scriba: "De Cleopatra regina fabulam scribo."

Scribe: "I am writing a story about Queen Cleopatra."

Pax in Aegypto post bella longa est. Aegyptus sub Romana pace vivit.

Peace exists in Egypt after long wars. Egypt lives under Roman peace.

Aegyptius: "Pace nunc fruimur, sub Romano imperio."

An Egyptian: "We now enjoy peace under the Roman Empire."

Romani semper de Cleopatra et Caesar loquuntur. Eorum historia multos movet.

The Romans always speak of Cleopatra and Caesar. Their story moves many.

Romanus: "Cleopatra et Caesar magni fuerunt. Eorum amorem semper recordabimur."

A Roman: "Cleopatra and Caesar were great. We will always remember their love."

Monumenta Aegypti, ut pyramides et templa, magnifica sunt. Homines ea mirantur.

The monuments of Egypt, such as the pyramids and temples, are magnificent. People marvel at them.

Viator: "Aegypti monumenta sunt incredibilia!"

A traveler: "The monuments of Egypt are incredible!"

Cleopatra regina famosa est. Nomen eius semper in historia manet.

Cleopatra is a famous queen. Her name will always remain in history.

Historicus: "Cleopatra una reginarum famosarum est."

Historian: "Cleopatra is one of the most famous queens."

Caesar, dux magnus, in memoria Romanorum manet. Eius gesta laudantur.

Caesar, a great leader, remains in the memory of the Romans. His deeds are praised.

Romanus: "Caesar magnus imperator et dux fuit."

A Roman: "Caesar was a great general and leader."

Historiae Aegypti et Romae coniunctae sunt. Una magnam partem mundi efficiunt.

The histories of Egypt and Rome are connected. Together, they shape a large part of the world.

Magister: "Discite de Aegypto et Roma, quia historiae eorum coniunctae sunt."

A teacher: "Learn about Egypt and Rome, for their histories are intertwined."

Cleopatra et Caesar non moriuntur. In aeternum in mentibus hominum vivunt.

Cleopatra and Caesar do not die. They live forever in the minds of people.

Poeta: "Caesar et Cleopatra, amantes aeterni, in versibus nostris vivent."

A poet: "Caesar and Cleopatra, eternal lovers, will live on in our verses."

Victoria et Potentia

Capitulum Primum: Caesar Capturatur

Gaius Iulius Caesar iter per mare facit. Subito, piratae navigium eius aggrediuntur.

Gaius Julius Caesar is traveling by sea. Suddenly, pirates attack his ship.

Pirata: "Caesar, te captum habemus!"

Pirate: "Caesar, we have captured you!"

Caesar, intrepidus, piratis respondet: "Nolite me timere. Ego sum Caesar."

Caesar, fearless, responds to the pirates: "Do not fear me. I am Caesar."

Piratae, avidi, pecuniam a Caesare postulant.

The pirates, greedy, demand money from Caesar.

Pirata: "Pecuniam tuam nobis da!"

Pirate: "Give us your money!"

Caesar ridet et audaciter dicit: "Non solum pecuniam dabo, sed etiam plura promitto, si me liberaveritis."

Caesar laughs and boldly says: "Not only will I give you money, but I will also promise you more if you set me free."

Piratae, mirantes, Caesarem in nave sua tenent. Caesar cum piratis loquitur et imperat, quasi dux ipse esset.

The pirates, amazed, hold Caesar on their ship. Caesar speaks with the pirates and gives orders as if he were their leader.

Caesar: "Cibum et vinum mihi date. Etiam, in nave bene me tractate."

Caesar: "Give me food and wine. Also, treat me well on the ship."

Piratae, Caesaris audaciam mirantes, eum bene tractant. Interim, Caesar de libertate sua cogitat.

The pirates, amazed by Caesar's boldness, treat him well. Meanwhile, Caesar thinks about his freedom.

Caesar: "Volo me liberari. Promitto vobis pecuniam multam si me Romam redire sinatis."

Caesar: "I want to be freed. I promise you a lot of money if you let me return to Rome."

Piratae pecuniam magnam exspectant et de Caesare colloquuntur.

The pirates expect a large sum of money and talk about Caesar.

Pirata: "Caesar nobis pecuniam multam dabit. Fortasse eum liberare debemus."

Pirate: "Caesar will give us a lot of money. Perhaps we should free him."

Caesar, cum piratis collocutus, eis minatur: "Si me non liberaveritis, Romani venient et vos capient!"

Caesar, after talking with the pirates, threatens them: "If you do not free me, the Romans will come and capture you!"

Piratae, non credentes, ridere incipiunt.

The pirates, not believing him, start to laugh.

Pirata: "Tu, Caesar? Romani te liberare? Ridiculum!"

Pirate: "You, Caesar? The Romans will free you? Ridiculous!"

Caesar, confidens, in nave piratarum manet. Noctu, de libertate sua semper cogitat.

Caesar, confident, remains on the pirates' ship. At night, he constantly thinks about his freedom.

Capitulum Secundum: Caesar Liberatur

Post dies multos, amici Caesaris pecuniam piratis dant. Caesar liberatur.

After many days, Caesar's friends give money to the pirates. Caesar is freed.

Amicus: "Caesar, nunc liber es! Pecuniam piratis dedimus."

Friend: "Caesar, now you are free! We gave money to the pirates."

Caesar: "Gratias vobis ago. Nunc ad urbem redeo."

Caesar: "I thank you all. Now I return to the city."

Caesar Romam cum celeritate redit. Statim naves magnas parat.

Caesar quickly returns to Rome. Immediately, he prepares great ships.

Caesar: "Piratas invenire et capere volo. Naves parate!"

Caesar: "I want to find and capture the pirates. Prepare the ships!"

Milites fortissimi Caesarem sequuntur. Ad mare cum Caesare iter faciunt.

The bravest soldiers follow Caesar. They journey to the sea with Caesar.

Miles: "Dux Caesar, te sequimur. Piratas capiemus!"

Soldier: "Leader Caesar, we follow you. We will capture the pirates!"

Caesar et milites piratas in mari quaerunt. Mox piratas inveniunt.

Caesar and the soldiers search for the pirates at sea. Soon they find the pirates.

Caesar: "Ecce! Piratae sunt! Nunc eos capiamus!"

Caesar: "Look! There are the pirates! Now let's capture them!"

Pugna in mari fit. Caesar et milites piratas capiunt.

A battle takes place at sea. Caesar and the soldiers capture the pirates.

Pirata: "Heu! Capti sumus!"

Pirate: "Alas! We are captured!"

Caesar, victor, piratas Romam ducit. Piratae in carcere ponuntur.

Caesar, victorious, leads the pirates to Rome. The pirates are placed in prison.

Caesar: "Nunc in carcere estis. Iustitiam accipietis."

Caesar: "Now you are in prison. You will receive justice."

In foro Romano, Caesar de piratis iudicium fert. Multa populus audit.

In the Roman forum, Caesar gives judgment on the pirates. Many people listen.

Caesar: "Piratae poenam accipient. Iustitia Romana est."

Caesar: "The pirates will receive punishment. This is Roman justice."

Piratae poenam duram accipiunt. Caesar laudatus est.

The pirates receive a harsh punishment. Caesar is praised.

Populus: "Caesar, victor magnus es! Piratas vicisti!"

The people: "Caesar, you are a great victor! You have defeated the pirates!"

Caesar, victor, felix est. Populus eum laudat et celebrat.

Caesar, the victor, is happy. The people praise and celebrate him.

Capitulum Tertium: Caesar et Gloria

Iulius Caesar, post victoriam contra piratas, in Roma clarus est.

Julius Caesar, after his victory against the pirates, is famous in Rome.

Romanus: "Caesar, magnus dux es! Piratas vicisti!"

Roman: "Caesar, you are a great leader! You defeated the pirates!"

Caesar in foro de piratis narrat. Populus audit et laudat.

Caesar tells of the pirates in the forum. The people listen and praise him.

Caesar: "Piratas fortes vici. Romae semper serviam!"

Caesar: "I defeated the strong pirates. I will always serve Rome!"

Amici Caesaris cenam magnam celebrant. Gaudent de victoria.

Caesar's friends celebrate with a great feast. They rejoice over the victory.

Amicus: "Caesar, te celebramus! Victor es!"

Friend: "Caesar, we celebrate you! You are a victor!"

Caesar, in domo sua, de futuro cogitat. Magna in mente habet.

Caesar, in his home, thinks about the future. He has great plans in mind.

Caesar: "Novos hostes inveniam. Pro Roma pugnabo!"

Caesar: "I will find new enemies. I will fight for Rome!"

Caesar iterum iter facit. Ad novas terras navigat.

Caesar sets out on a journey again. He sails to new lands.

Nauta: "Caesar, ad terras novas navigamus!"

Sailor: "Caesar, we are sailing to new lands!"

In novis terris, Caesar novos hostes invenit et ad bellum parat.

In new lands, Caesar finds new enemies and prepares for war.

Caesar: "Hostes novi sunt. Parati ad bellum sumus!"

Caesar: "There are new enemies. We are ready for war!"

Caesar, dux fortis, milites Romanos ad pugnam docet.

Caesar, the strong leader, teaches the Roman soldiers how to fight.

Caesar: "Milites, sic pugnabitis. Me sequimini!"

Caesar: "Soldiers, you will fight like this. Follow me!"

Sub duce Caesar, milites multas victorias habent. Caesar laudatur.

Under Caesar's leadership, the soldiers achieve many victories. Caesar is praised.

Miles: "Caesar, dux fortis es! Te sequimur!"

Soldier: "Caesar, you are a strong leader! We follow you!"

Caesar cum gloria Romam redit. Populus eum exspectat.

Caesar returns to Rome with glory. The people are waiting for him.

Romanus: "Ecce! Caesar redit. Multas victorias habet!"

Roman: "Look! Caesar returns. He has many victories!"

In Roma, Caesar triumphum magnificum habet. Viae plenae sunt.

In Rome, Caesar has a magnificent triumph. The streets are full.

Populus: "Caesar, heros Romanus es! Triumphum tuum laudamus!"

The people: "Caesar, you are a Roman hero! We praise your triumph!"

Caesar, in corde Romae, heros magnus est. Omnes eum amant.

Caesar, in the heart of Rome, is a great hero. Everyone loves him.

Capitulum Quartum: Caesar et Senatus

Iulius Caesar in senatu Romano stat et loquitur.

Julius Caesar stands in the Roman Senate and speaks.

Caesar: "Piratas superavi. Nunc de pace Romae cogito."

Caesar: "I have defeated the pirates. Now I think of peace for Rome."

Senatores, audientes, Caesarem magnopere laudant.

The senators, listening, greatly praise Caesar.

Senator: "Caesar, magnus dux es! Roma tibi gratias agit."

Senator: "Caesar, you are a great leader! Rome thanks you."

Caesar multas leges novas proponit. Nonnulli senatores dubitant.

Caesar proposes many new laws. Some senators have doubts.

Senator: "Non omnes leges tuae nobis placent, Caesar."

Senator: "Not all of your laws please us, Caesar."

Sed Caesar, populo Romano placens, multos amicos in senatu habet.

But Caesar, pleasing the Roman people, has many friends in the Senate.

Amicus Caesaris: "Caesar, tecum sumus. Leges tuae bonae sunt."

Friend of Caesar: "Caesar, we are with you. Your laws are good."

Tamen Caesar etiam inimicos habet. Non omnes eum amant.

However, Caesar also has enemies. Not everyone loves him.

Inimicus Caesaris: "Caesar nimis potens est. Cauti esse debemus."

Enemy of Caesar: "Caesar is too powerful. We must be cautious."

Caesar, cum prudentia, de pace et securitate Romae cogitat.

Caesar, with wisdom, thinks about peace and security for Rome.

Caesar: "Pax et securitas Romae sunt maxime importantia."

Caesar: "Peace and security for Rome are of the utmost importance."

Caesar et senatores de futuris rebus Romae consiliunt.

Caesar and the senators deliberate on Rome's future affairs.

Senator: "Quid agemus de provinciis novis?"

Senator: "What shall we do about the new provinces?"

Caesar in Roma manet et ad novas res parat. Semper vigilans est.

Caesar stays in Rome and prepares for new matters. He is always vigilant.

Caesar: "Semper Romae serviam. Novas res paro."

Caesar: "I will always serve Rome. I am preparing new things."

Caesar et senatus post longam consultationem finiunt. Roma progreditur.

Caesar and the Senate finish after a long consultation. Rome advances.

Capitulum Quintum: Caesar et Populus

Iulius Caesar, in corde Romae, populum amat et pro eis curat.

Julius Caesar, in the heart of Rome, loves the people and cares for them.

Caesar: "Populus Romanus mihi carus est. Eorum bene esse volo."

Caesar: "The Roman people are dear to me. I want their well-being."

Caesar in foro Romano stat et ad populum loquitur.

Caesar stands in the Roman Forum and speaks to the people.

Caesar: "Pacem et securitatem vobis promitto. Romae semper serviam."

Caesar: "I promise you peace and security. I will always serve Rome."

Populus, audientes Caesarem, eum magnopere laudat.

The people, hearing Caesar, greatly praise him.

Romanus: "Caesar, te amamus! Pro nobis curas!"

Roman: "Caesar, we love you! You care for us!"

Caesar dona magnifica populo dat. Ludos et spectacula parat.

Caesar gives great gifts to the people. He prepares games and shows.

Caesar: "Hodie ludos magnos vobis do. Gaudeamus!"

Caesar: "Today I give you great games. Let us rejoice!"

Populus in foro festa celebrat. Ludi et musica ubique sunt.

The people celebrate festivals in the Forum. Games and music are everywhere.

Romanus: "Ecce! Ludi et festa! Caesar nos amat!"

Roman: "Look! Games and festivities! Caesar loves us!"

Caesar, gaudio plenus, cum populo festum celebrat.

Caesar, full of joy, celebrates the festival with the people.

Caesar: "Una cum vobis gaudeo. Romani sumus!"

Caesar: "I rejoice with you all. We are Romans!"

Caesar de plebe, pauperibus Romae, curat. Cibum eis distribuit.

Caesar cares for the common people, the poor of Rome. He distributes food to them.

Caesar: "Nemo in Roma esuriet. Cibum pauperibus do."

Caesar: "No one in Rome will go hungry. I give food to the poor."

Populus Romanus Caesarem amat. Eum herum suum vocant.

The Roman people love Caesar. They call him their lord.

Romanus: "Caesar, dux noster et protector! Te sequimur!"

Roman: "Caesar, our leader and protector! We follow you!"

Caesar, magnus dux, populum ducit. Eum populus fideliter sequitur.

Caesar, the great leader, leads the people. The people faithfully follow him.

Romanus: "Quo Caesar it, nos sequimur. Ei confidimus!"

Roman: "Where Caesar goes, we follow. We trust him!"

Caesar et populus Romani, una, magni sunt. Roma floret.

Caesar and the Roman people, together, are great. Rome flourishes.

Capitulum Sextum: Caesar Militat

Iulius Caesar, magnus dux Romanorum, ad bellum iter facit.

Julius Caesar, the great leader of the Romans, sets out for war.

Caesar: "Ad bellum imus. Victoria nostra erit!"

Caesar: "We go to war. Victory will be ours!"

Caesar exercitum Romanum ducit. Milites eum sequuntur.

Caesar leads the Roman army. The soldiers follow him.

Miles: "Te, Caesar, sequimur! Ad victoriam!"

Soldier: "We follow you, Caesar! To victory!"

Hostes Romani proelium parant. Armantur et castra ponunt.

The Roman enemies prepare for battle. They arm themselves and set up camp.

Hostis: "Romani veniunt. Parati esse debemus!"

Enemy: "The Romans are coming. We must be ready!"

Caesar, prope hostes, castra Romana ponit. Milites parati sunt.

Caesar sets up the Roman camp near the enemy. The soldiers are ready.

Caesar: "Milites, ad proelium parati estote. Hodie pugnabimus!"

Caesar: "Soldiers, be ready for battle. Today we will fight!"

Caesar, audacter, hostes ad proelium provocat. Bellum incipit.

Caesar boldly challenges the enemies to battle. The war begins.

Caesar: "Hostes, venite! Romani non timent!"

Caesar: "Enemies, come! The Romans are not afraid!"

In proelio, Caesar fortiter pugnat. Milites eum sequuntur.

In battle, Caesar fights bravely. The soldiers follow him.

Caesar: "Pro Roma pugnate! Fortes estote!"

Caesar: "Fight for Rome! Be strong!"

Hostes, Romana virtute superati, fugam capiunt.

The enemies, overcome by Roman bravery, flee.

Miles: "Hostes fugiunt! Victoria nostra est!"

Soldier: "The enemies are fleeing! Victory is ours!"

Caesar, victor, laetissimus est. Milites eum laudant.

Caesar, victorious, is very happy. The soldiers praise him.

Miles: "Caesar, victoria tua est! Te laudamus!"

Soldier: "Caesar, the victory is yours! We praise you!"

Caesar captivos ex hostibus accipit et clementer agit.

Caesar accepts captives from the enemies and acts mercifully.

Caesar: "Captivi, nunc Romani estis. Bene vos tractabimus."

Caesar: "Captives, now you are Romans. We will treat you well."

Caesar, post victoriam, ad aliam terram movet. Semper pugnat.

Caesar, after the victory, moves to another land. He always fights.

Caesar: "Ad aliam terram imus. Semper victores erimus!"

Caesar: "We go to another land. We will always be victors!"

Caesar, semper victor, ad Romam redit. Triumphum habet.

Caesar, always victorious, returns to Rome. He has a triumph.

Romanus: "Caesar redit! Triumphum eius celebramus!"

Roman: "Caesar returns! We celebrate his triumph!"

Capitulum Septimum: Caesar et Politica

Iulius Caesar, post victorias, de re publica Romana multum cogitat.

Julius Caesar, after his victories, thinks much about the Roman Republic.

Caesar: "Roma magnam potentiam habet. Pro re publica laborabo."

Caesar: "Rome has great power. I will work for the Republic."

Caesar cum senatoribus Romae loquitur. Vult consul fieri.

Caesar speaks with the senators in Rome. He wants to become consul.

Caesar: "Senatores, consul fieri volo. Pro Roma laborare possum."

Caesar: "Senators, I want to become consul. I can work for Rome."

Non omnes senatores Caesarem amant. Aliqui inimici sunt.

Not all the senators love Caesar. Some are his enemies.

Inimicus: "Caesar nimis potens est. Eum oppugnare debemus."

Enemy: "Caesar is too powerful. We must oppose him."

Caesar, tamen, multos amicos habet. Eum in senatu sustinent.

Caesar, however, has many friends. They support him in the Senate.

Amicus: "Caesar, te adiuvabimus. Consul fieri potes!"

Friend: "Caesar, we will help you. You can become consul!"

Caesar in senatu multas disputationes habet. Senatum vincit.

Caesar has many debates in the Senate. He overcomes the Senate.

Senator: "Caesar consulatum meruit. Ei faveamus!"

Senator: "Caesar has earned the consulship. Let us support him!"

Caesar, post multam contentionem, consul fit. Multas leges novas facit.

Caesar, after much struggle, becomes consul. He makes many new laws.

Caesar: "Leges novas pro populo Romano facio."

Caesar: "I make new laws for the Roman people."

Populus Romanus Caesarem amat. Ei placet quia populo curat.

The Roman people love Caesar. They like him because he cares for the people.

Romanus: "Caesar, bonum consulem te esse credimus!"

Roman: "Caesar, we believe you are a good consul!"

Inimici Caesarem timent. Potentiam eius vident.

Caesar's enemies fear him. They see his power.

Inimicus: "Caesar nimis potens fit. Timemus quid faciet."

Enemy: "Caesar is becoming too powerful. We fear what he will do."

Caesar, tamen, potentiam magnam habet. Populo semper cum est.

Caesar, however, has great power. He is always with the people.

Caesar: "Cum populo Romano sum. Eorum bene esse volo."

Caesar: "I am with the Roman people. I want their well-being."

Caesar et senatus de rebus magnis agunt. Roma progreditur.

Caesar and the Senate deal with important matters. Rome progresses.

Senator: "Caesar et senatus pro Roma laborant."

Senator: "Caesar and the Senate work for Rome."

In Roma, Caesar valde potens est. Multa pro Roma facit.

In Rome, Caesar is very powerful. He does much for Rome.

Romanus: "Caesar Romae est dux magnus. Eum sequimur!"

Roman: "Caesar is a great leader of Rome. We follow him!"

Caesar et populus Romani uniti sunt. Una fortiores sunt.

Caesar and the Roman people are united. Together they are stronger.

Caesar: "Romani, una sumus fortiores. Ad maiora aspiciamus!"

Caesar: "Romans, together we are stronger. Let us aim for greater things!"

Capitulum Octavum: Caesar et Futurum

Iulius Caesar, magnus dux Romanus, de futuro Romae magnae cogitat.

Julius Caesar, the great Roman leader, thinks about the future of great Rome.

Caesar: "Roma futura magnam potentiam habebit. Eam amplificare volo."

Caesar: "Future Rome will have great power. I want to expand it."

Caesar ad novas terras it. Multas expeditiones facit.

Caesar goes to new lands. He carries out many expeditions.

Caesar: "Ad novas terras navigamus. Crescat Roma!"

Caesar: "We sail to new lands. Let Rome grow!"

In his terris, Caesar multos hostes vincit. Victoriae multae sunt.

In these lands, Caesar defeats many enemies. There are many victories.

Miles: "Caesar, te duce, hostes vincimus! Roma invicta est!"

Soldier: "Caesar, with you as our leader, we defeat the enemies! Rome is undefeated!"

Caesar novas vias per imperium Romanum facit. Commercium crescit.

Caesar builds new roads throughout the Roman Empire. Trade increases.

Architectus: "Caesar, viae novae urbes connectunt. Bonum opus est!"

Architect: "Caesar, the new roads connect the cities. It is good work!"

Urbes novas aedificat. Roma non solum urbs est, sed etiam imperium.

He builds new cities. Rome is not only a city, but also an empire.

Civis: "Urbes novae crescunt. Roma ubique est!"

Citizen: "New cities are growing. Rome is everywhere!"

Caesar populum Romanum educat. Scholas aedificat.

Caesar educates the Roman people. He builds schools.

Praeceptor: "Caesar, gratias tibi! Nunc liberi melius discunt."

Teacher: "Caesar, thank you! Now the children learn better."

Scientiam et artes promovet. Roma est centrum sapientiae.

He promotes science and the arts. Rome is a center of wisdom.

Scientist: "Caesar nos adiuvat. Scientia floret!"

Scientist: "Caesar helps us. Knowledge is flourishing!"

Caesar bellum contra piratas narrat. Populus admiratur.

Caesar tells the story of his war against the pirates. The people admire him.

Romanus: "Caesar, historia tua mirabilis est! Piratas vincebas!"

Roman: "Caesar, your story is amazing! You defeated the pirates!"

Populus Romanus Caesarem amat. Eum herum suum vocant.

The Roman people love Caesar. They call him their master.

Romanus: "Caesar, semper te amabimus! Dux magnus es!"

Roman: "Caesar, we will always love you! You are a great leader!"

Caesar, in historia, magnus est. Nomen eius non obliviscitur.

Caesar is great in history. His name is not forgotten.

Historicus: "Caesar in historia semper erit. Magnus dux fuit."

Historian: "Caesar will always be in history. He was a great leader."

Caesar Romam magnam facit. Urbs est potentissima.

Caesar makes Rome great. The city is the most powerful.

Architectus: "Roma, sub Caesare, magnificatur. Urbs aeterna est!"

Architect: "Rome, under Caesar, is made magnificent. It is the eternal city!"

Caesar in historia manet. Exemplum virtutis et sapientiae est.

Caesar remains in history. He is an example of virtue and wisdom.

Magister: "Discipuli, Caesarem imitamini. Fortis et sapiens fuit."

Teacher: "Students, imitate Caesar. He was strong and wise."

In cordibus Romanorum, Caesar semper est. Memoria eius manet.

In the hearts of Romans, Caesar is always present. His memory remains.

Romanus: "Caesar, in corde nostro semper eris. Memoria tua aeterna est!"

Roman: "Caesar, you will always be in our hearts. Your memory is eternal!"

Tiberius Imperator

Capitulum Primum: Ascensus Tiberii

Tiberius, Augusti privignus, imperator Romanorum factus est. "Imperator ero," Tiberius in palatio cogitabat.

Tiberius, the stepson of Augustus, became the emperor of the Romans. "I will be emperor," Tiberius thought in the palace.

In politica et militaria arte Tiberius eruditus erat. "Militiae et rei publicae studui," Tiberius amico suo dixit.

Tiberius was educated in the art of politics and military. "I have studied military and public affairs," Tiberius said to his friend.

Augustus Tiberium successorem nominavit. "Tiberius post me regnabit," Augustus in senatu pronuntiavit.

Augustus named Tiberius as his successor. "Tiberius will reign after me," Augustus proclaimed in the senate.

Tiberius de potestate acceptanda dubitabat. "Num imperium accipiam?" Tiberius se ipsum interrogabat.

Tiberius hesitated about accepting power. "Shall I take the empire?" Tiberius asked himself.

Senatus Romanus Tiberium imperatorem confirmavit. "Tiberium confirmamus," princeps senator dixit.

The Roman Senate confirmed Tiberius as emperor. "We confirm Tiberius," the chief senator said.

Initio regni sui, Tiberius moderationem ostendebat. "Moderate regnabo," Tiberius ad senatorem dixit.

At the beginning of his reign, Tiberius showed moderation. "I will rule moderately," Tiberius said to the senator.

Populus Romanus Tiberii regnum suscepit. "Tiberium accipimus," populus in foro clamavit.

The Roman people accepted Tiberius' reign. "We accept Tiberius," the people shouted in the forum.

Tiberius Germaniam et Pannoniam stabilivit. "Germaniam et Pannoniam pacabo," Tiberius dixit.

Tiberius stabilized Germany and Pannonia. "I will bring peace to Germany and Pannonia," Tiberius said.

Regni sui initium Tiberius in pace et securitate posuit. "Pacem et securitatem quaero," Tiberius in consilio dixit.

Tiberius established the beginning of his reign in peace and security. "I seek peace and security," Tiberius said in the council.

Seianus, praefectus praetorio, consiliarius Tiberii factus est. "Seiane, mihi consiliarius eris," Tiberius Seiano dixit.

Sejanus, the praetorian prefect, became Tiberius' advisor. "Sejanus, you will be my advisor," Tiberius said to Sejanus.

Tiberius Romae auctoritatem firmiter tenebat. "Roma sub me florebit," Tiberius in curia dixit.

Tiberius held authority in Rome firmly. "Rome will flourish under me," Tiberius said in the senate.

Tiberius leges et iustitiam in imperio promovebat. "Leges et iustitiam promovebo," Tiberius ad iudices dixit.

Tiberius promoted laws and justice in the empire. "I will promote laws and justice," Tiberius said to the judges.

Agrippina, Tiberii privigna, de eius potestate sollicita erat. "Quid Tiberius agit?" Agrippina amicae suae dixit.

Agrippina, the stepdaughter of Tiberius, was worried about his power. "What is Tiberius doing?" Agrippina said to her friend.

Tiberius filio suo, Druso, confidebat. "Druse, confido in te," Tiberius ad filium suum dixit.

Tiberius trusted his son, Drusus. "Drusus, I trust you," Tiberius said to his son.

Rumores de Tiberii crudelitate inter populum coeperunt. "Tiberius crudelis est," civis in foro susurrabat.

Rumors of Tiberius' cruelty began to spread among the people. "Tiberius is cruel," a citizen whispered in the forum.

In hoc capitulo, narratur ascensus Tiberii ad imperium Romanorum post Augustum, eius eruditio in politica et militaria arte, dubitationes eius de potestate, et confirmatio senatus. Populus eius regnum suscepit, et Tiberius initium pacificum et securum regni sui posuit, cum Seiano ut consiliario. Rumores de eius crudelitate coeperunt, cum Agrippina et filius eius, Drusus, in historia eius partes habent.

In this chapter, the rise of Tiberius to the Roman Empire after Augustus is narrated, along with his education in political and military arts, his doubts about power, and the confirmation by the senate. The people accepted his reign, and Tiberius laid the peaceful and secure foundation of his reign, with Sejanus as his advisor. Rumors of his cruelty began to spread, while Agrippina and his son Drusus played roles in his story.

Capitulum Secundum: Tiberius et Seianus

Seianus, vir ambitiosus, in curia Romana potentiam augere coepit. "Potentiam meam in curia augere volo," Seianus in secreto cogitabat.

Sejanus, an ambitious man, began to increase his power in the Roman court. "I want to increase my power in the court," Sejanus thought secretly.

Tiberius imperator Seiano magis magisque confidebat. "Seiane, tua consilia mihi utilia sunt," Tiberius ad Seianum dixit.

Emperor Tiberius trusted Sejanus more and more. "Sejanus, your advice is useful to me," Tiberius said to Sejanus.

Seianus, potestate sua uti cupiens, adversarios politicos eliminare conatus est. "Adversarios meos removebo," Seianus astute sibi dixit.

Sejanus, eager to use his power, attempted to eliminate his political opponents. "I will remove my enemies," Sejanus cunningly said to himself.

Tiberius, imperii curis fessus, Romae minus saepe apparebat. "Romae minus saepe ero," Tiberius ad consiliarium suum dixit.

Tiberius, tired of the cares of the empire, appeared in Rome less frequently. "I will be in Rome less often," Tiberius said to his advisor.

Seianus Agrippinam, Tiberii privignam, et filios eius suspectos habebat. "Agrippina et liberi eius mihi suspecti sunt," Seianus in concilio susurrabat.

Sejanus regarded Agrippina, Tiberius's stepdaughter, and her children as suspicious. "Agrippina and her children are suspicious to me," Sejanus whispered in council.

Tiberius in insulam Capream secessit, Seiano rebus Romanis praeposito. "Seiane, rebus Romanis praeside," Tiberius, Capream navigans, mandavit.

Tiberius withdrew to the island of Capri, putting Sejanus in charge of Roman affairs. "Sejanus, oversee Roman affairs," Tiberius commanded as he sailed to Capri.

In senatu Romano, Seianus magis influens factus est. "In senatu nunc magis valeo," Seianus, ambitiosus, cogitabat.

In the Roman Senate, Sejanus became more influential. "I am now more powerful in the Senate," Sejanus thought ambitiously.

Tiberius, Capreae remotus, per litteras imperium administrabat. "Per litteras regnabo," Tiberius scribens dixit.

Tiberius, distant in Capri, governed the empire through letters. "I will rule by letters," Tiberius said as he wrote.

Seianus Germanicum, Tiberii nepotem, ut inimicum habebat. "Germanicus mihi adversarius est," Seianus in secreto cogitabat.

Sejanus considered Germanicus, Tiberius's nephew, an enemy. "Germanicus is my adversary," Sejanus thought secretly.

Tiberius, nuntiis de Seiani ambitionibus allatis, sollicitus erat. "Seianus me superare conatur?" Tiberius anxius cogitabat.

Tiberius, hearing reports of Sejanus's ambitions, was troubled. "Is Sejanus trying to surpass me?" Tiberius anxiously thought.

Seianus Agrippinam et filios eius rei publicae adversos esse accusavit. "Agrippinam et liberos eius accusabo," Seianus consilio suo dixit.

Sejanus accused Agrippina and her children of being enemies of the state. "I will accuse Agrippina and her children," Sejanus said to his counsel.

Tiberius, Seiani verbis deceptus, consiliis eius credebat. "Seiani consilia sequar," Tiberius in palatio suo dixit.

Tiberius, deceived by Sejanus's words, trusted his counsel. "I will follow Sejanus's advice," Tiberius said in his palace.

Agrippina et filii eius in exilium missi sunt, Seiani accusationibus credentibus. "In exilium eunt," Seianus, victor, inquit.

Agrippina and her children were sent into exile, with people believing Sejanus's accusations. "They are going into exile," Sejanus said triumphantly.

Seianus, potestate corruptus, eam ad suos fines abusus est. "Potestate mea utar," Seianus, potentia ebrius, dixit.

Sejanus, corrupted by power, abused it for his own ends. "I will use my power," Sejanus, drunk with power, said.

Tiberius, tandem, de Seiani veris intentionibus suspicatus est. "Seianus me fallit?" Tiberius, suspectus, cogitabat.

Tiberius, at last, began to suspect Sejanus's true intentions. "Is Sejanus deceiving me?" Tiberius thought, suspicious.

In hoc capitulo, narratur ascensus Seiani ad potentiam in curia Romana et fiducia, quam Tiberius in eum posuit. Seianus, ambitione ductus, adversarios politicos eliminare conatus est et Agrippinam ac filios eius suspectos habuit. Tiberius, sollicitudinibus imperii affectus, in insulam Capream secessit, et Seianus in rebus Romanis potentiam exercuit. Tamen, Tiberius tandem de Seiani veris intentionibus suspicatus est.

This chapter tells of Sejanus's rise to power in the Roman court and the trust Tiberius placed in him. Sejanus, driven by ambition, attempted to eliminate political opponents and regarded Agrippina and her children with suspicion. Tiberius, overwhelmed by the burdens of the empire, withdrew to the island of Capri, and Sejanus exercised power over Roman affairs. However, Tiberius eventually began to suspect Sejanus's true intentions.

Capitulum Tertium: Casus Seiani

Tiberius, imperator Romanus, Seiani veram naturam intellegens, consilium contra eum cepit. "Seiani veram naturam nunc video," Tiberius in secreto cogitabat.

Tiberius, the Roman emperor, realizing the true nature of Sejanus, devised a plan against him. "Now I see the true nature of Sejanus," Tiberius thought in secret.

Seianus, praefectus praetorio, ad summum honorem in statu Romano aspirabat. "Summum honorem attingam," Seianus ambitiose sibi dixit.

Sejanus, the prefect of the praetorian guard, aspired to the highest honor in the Roman state. "I will attain the highest honor," Sejanus ambitiously said to himself.

Tiberius, callidus et cautus, occulte contra Seianum moliri coepit. "Contra Seianum agam," Tiberius in palatio suo meditatus est.

Tiberius, cunning and cautious, secretly began to plot against Sejanus. "I will act against Sejanus," Tiberius meditated in his palace.

Tiberius litteras ad senatum Romanum misit, Seianum variis criminibus accusans. "Seianum accuso," Tiberius scribens mandavit.

Tiberius sent letters to the Roman Senate, accusing Sejanus of various crimes. "I accuse Sejanus," Tiberius wrote and commanded.

Seianus, nuntiis Tiberii deceptus, confidens in senatum Romae venit. "Nihil timeo," Seianus ingressus senatum dixit.

Sejanus, deceived by Tiberius's messages, confidently went to the Roman Senate. "I fear nothing," Sejanus said as he entered the Senate.

In senatu, Seianus repente a senatoribus accusatus est. "Seiane, accusaris!" princeps senator exclamavit.

In the Senate, Sejanus was suddenly accused by the senators. "Sejanus, you are accused!" the chief senator exclaimed.

Senatus Romanus, Seiani crimina audiens, eum statim condemnavit. "Seianum condemnamus," senatores in concilio dixerunt.

The Roman Senate, hearing Sejanus's crimes, immediately condemned him. "We condemn Sejanus," the senators said in council.

Seianus a custodibus Romanis captus est, sine ulla defensione. "Captus es," custos Romanus ad Seianum dixit.

Sejanus was captured by Roman guards, without any defense. "You are captured," a Roman guard said to Sejanus.

Populus Romanus, Seiani casu audito, gavisus est, tyrannidem eius odiens. "Seianus captus est!" populus in foris clamavit.

The Roman people, hearing of Sejanus's downfall, rejoiced, hating his tyranny. "Sejanus has been captured!" the people shouted in the forums.

Seianus in carcere necatus est, senatus iudicio. "Seianus necatus est," nuntius per urbem cucurrit.

Sejanus was killed in prison by the judgment of the Senate. "Sejanus has been killed," a messenger ran through the city announcing.

Tiberius, post Seiani casum, potentiam in Roma restituit. "Roma sub mea potestate est," Tiberius in senatu dixit.

Tiberius, after Sejanus's fall, restored his power in Rome. "Rome is under my control," Tiberius said in the Senate.

Tiberius novos consiliarios elegit, fideles et probos. "Novos consiliarios eligo," Tiberius ad consiliarium suum dixit.

Tiberius chose new advisors, loyal and trustworthy. "I choose new advisors," Tiberius said to his counselor.

Leges duriores contra proditores et conspiratores Tiberius promulgavit. "Leges duriores contra proditores statuam," Tiberius in curia pronuntiavit.

Tiberius enacted stricter laws against traitors and conspirators. "I will establish stricter laws against traitors," Tiberius announced in the Senate.

Imperium suum Tiberius firmiter tenuit, auctoritate sua utendo. "Imperium meum firmiter tenebo," Tiberius in consilio suo affirmavit.

Tiberius held his empire firmly, using his authority. "I will hold my empire firmly," Tiberius affirmed in his council.

Tiberius, Seiani comites et sequaces persecutus est, securitatem suam quaerens. "Seiani comites persequar," Tiberius imperator decrevit.

Tiberius pursued Sejanus's companions and followers, seeking his own security. "I will pursue Sejanus's companions," Tiberius, the emperor, decreed.

In hoc capitulo, narratur casus Seiani, qui potentiam in statu Romano ad summum gradum per ambitionem suam quaesivit, sed a Tiberio, imperatore astuto, deceptus et tandem captus atque necatus est. Tiberius, post Seiani casum, potentiam suam in Roma restituit et imperium suum firmiter tenuit.

This chapter narrates the fall of Sejanus, who sought the highest power in the Roman state through his ambition, but was deceived by the cunning Emperor Tiberius, eventually being captured and killed. After Sejanus's fall, Tiberius restored his power in Rome and held his empire firmly.

Capitulum Quartum: Tiberii Anni Tardi

Tiberius, imperator Romanus, in insula Capreae diutius manebat. "Capreae manebam," Tiberius solus in villa sua dixit.

Tiberius, the Roman emperor, stayed on the island of Capri for a long time. "I was staying in Capri," Tiberius said alone in his villa.

De imperio Romano per litteras et nuntios agebat, Roma remota. "Per litteras regnam," Tiberius ad scribam suum mandavit.

He managed the Roman Empire through letters and messengers, far from Rome. "I will rule through letters," Tiberius instructed his scribe.

De re publica Romanorum sollicitus erat, sed a populo secedebat. "De republica sollicitus sum," Tiberius in meditatione inquit.

He was concerned about the Roman Republic but withdrew from the people. "I am worried about the Republic," Tiberius said in contemplation.

Legatos et senatores Romae saepius interrogabat, curam rerum gestarum habens. "Quid Romae agitur?" Tiberius per litteras quaesivit.

He often questioned envoys and senators in Rome, keeping an eye on events. "What is happening in Rome?" Tiberius asked through letters.

In suspicionem et metum incidit, de conspirationibus timens. "Coniurationes ubique sunt," Tiberius anxius cogitabat.

He fell into suspicion and fear, worried about conspiracies. "There are conspiracies everywhere," Tiberius anxiously thought.

Accusationes contra senatores et equites audivit, saepe infundatas. "Senatores equitesque suspecti sunt," Tiberius ad consiliarium suum dixit.

He heard accusations against senators and knights, often unfounded. "Senators and knights are suspect," Tiberius said to his advisor.

Delatores, qui accusationes portabant, ad usum proprium adhibebat. "Delatores mihi utiles sunt," Tiberius in secreto colloquio dixit.

He used informers, who brought accusations, for his own purposes. "Informers are useful to me," Tiberius said in a secret conversation.

Tiberius mortem Drusi, filii sui, profunde lugebat. "Druse, me desideras," Tiberius in luctu dixit.

Tiberius deeply mourned the death of his son Drusus. "Drusus, do you miss me?" Tiberius said in his grief.

In politica et militaria Roma minus operosus erat, se a curis publicis removens. "Minus in rebus publicis agam," Tiberius decrevit.

He was less active in Roman politics and military matters, withdrawing from public affairs. "I will engage less in public matters," Tiberius decreed.

Curam rerum Romanarum habebat, sed a distante. "Rerum Romanarum curam habeo," Tiberius ad amicum epistulam scripsit.

He cared for Roman affairs, but from a distance. "I care for Roman affairs," Tiberius wrote in a letter to a friend.

Iustitiam et leges promovere pergebat, sed cum severitate. "Iustitiam legesque servabo," Tiberius in iudicio dixit.

He continued to promote justice and laws, but with severity. "I will uphold justice and laws," Tiberius said in court.

Auctoritate et potentia usus est, imperium suum firmando. "Potentia mea firma est," Tiberius in solitudine sua dixit.

He used authority and power, strengthening his empire. "My power is firm," Tiberius said in his solitude.

In senatu et populo timebatur, metus eius potentiam augens. "Tiberius timetur," senator Romanus ad alium susurravit.

He was feared by the Senate and the people, his fear increasing his power. "Tiberius is feared," a Roman senator whispered to another.

Imperium sine oppositione tenebat, auctoritate absoluta utendo. "Nulla mihi oppositio est," Tiberius, confidenter, inquit.

He held the empire without opposition, using absolute authority. "There is no opposition to me," Tiberius said confidently.

Morbus et senectute laborabat, valetudine sua deficiente. "Senectus me affligit," Tiberius, infirmus, cogitabat.

He suffered from illness and old age, with his health declining. "Old age afflicts me," Tiberius, weak, thought.

In hoc capitulo, narratur de Tiberii ultimis annis, in quibus in insula Capreae morabatur et imperium Romanum a longinquo administrabat. Tiberius, suspicionibus et metu motus, delatores adhibuit et in politica minus operosus fuit. Mortem filii sui lugebat et in senectute sua de valetudine laborabat, cum imperium sine oppositione teneret.

This chapter narrates the final years of Tiberius, during which he resided on the island of Capri and managed the Roman Empire from afar. Motivated by suspicion and fear, Tiberius employed informers and was less active in politics. He mourned the death of his son and struggled with his health in old age, while maintaining the empire without opposition.

Capitulum Quintum: Finis Regni Tiberii

Tiberius, aetate et morbo affectus, finem vitae suae appropinquabat. "Vita mea finem appropinquat," Tiberius in villa sua Capreae cogitabat.

Tiberius, affected by age and illness, was approaching the end of his life. "My life is nearing its end," Tiberius thought in his villa at Capri.

In insula Capreae, Tiberius, imperator Romanorum, diem ultimum obiit. "Imperator mortuus est," nuntius in Roma divulgavit.

On the island of Capri, Tiberius, the emperor of the Romans, passed away. "The emperor is dead," a messenger announced in Rome.

Tiberius Gaium Caligulam, nepotem suum, ut successorem reliquit. "Caligula me sequetur," Tiberius in testamento suo scripsit.

Tiberius left Gaius Caligula, his nephew, as his successor. "Caligula will follow me," Tiberius wrote in his will.

Longum et turbulentum imperium Tiberii finitum est, multis mutationibus rei publicae plenum. "Longum regnum fuit," senator Romanus ad collegam suum dixit.

Tiberius's long and turbulent reign came to an end, filled with many changes to the state. "It was a long reign," a Roman senator said to his colleague.

In historia Romana, Tiberius figura complexa et ambigua manet. "Tiberius multas facies habuit," historiographus Romanus in libro suo scripsit.

In Roman history, Tiberius remains a complex and ambiguous figure. "Tiberius had many faces," a Roman historian wrote in his book.

Post mortem, Tiberius a senatu Romanorum deificatus est, more Romanorum. "Tiberium inter deos ponemus," sacerdos Romanus in senatu dixit.

After his death, Tiberius was deified by the Roman Senate, according to Roman custom. "We will place Tiberius among the gods," a Roman priest said in the Senate.

Mors Tiberii mixtas reactiones inter populum Romanum habuit. "Nonne bene regnavit?" civis Romanus in foro interrogavit.

The death of Tiberius provoked mixed reactions among the Roman people. "Did he not rule well?" a Roman citizen asked in the forum.

Tiberius imperium Romanum per tempora sua stabilivit, multas provincias pacificans. "Imperium stabilivit," legatus Romanus in concilio dixit.

Tiberius stabilized the Roman Empire during his reign, pacifying many provinces. "He stabilized the empire," a Roman envoy said in council.

In arte militari et administratione, Tiberius rem publicam Romanam effecit. "Militaria et administrativa bene egit," generalis Romanus ad milites suos inquit.

In military and administrative matters, Tiberius strengthened the Roman state. "He handled military and administrative affairs well," a Roman general said to his soldiers.

Multos monumentos et aedificia in Roma Tiberius reliquit, urbi decorem addens. "Videte, quae Tiberius aedificavit," turista Romanus amico suo demonstravit.

Tiberius left behind many monuments and buildings in Rome, adding beauty to the city. "Look at what Tiberius built," a Roman tourist showed his friend.

In memoria populi Romani, Tiberius variabiliter manet, nonnullis admiratus, aliis criticatus. "Quid de Tiberio cogitas?" civis Romanus ad amicum suum in via rogavit.

In the memory of the Roman people, Tiberius remains seen in various ways, admired by some, criticized by others. "What do you think of Tiberius?" a Roman citizen asked his friend on the street.

Tiberius, imperator Romanus, in annalibus Romanis pro suis actis et regno scribitur. "De Tiberio in annalibus legimus," magister in schola Romana discipulis suis dixit.

Tiberius, the Roman emperor, is recorded in Roman annals for his deeds and reign. "We read about Tiberius in the annals," a teacher in a Roman school told his students.

Rei publicae Romanorum, Tiberius multum contribuit, leges et administrationem promovens. "Tiberius rei publicae multum dedit," senator in curia loquebatur.

To the Roman state, Tiberius contributed greatly, promoting laws and administration. "Tiberius gave much to the Republic," a senator said in the Senate.

Cum Tiberio mortuo, nova aetas in imperio Romano coepit, multa mutatione signata. "Nova aetas incipit," civis Romanus in foro cum aliis colloquebatur.

With Tiberius's death, a new era began in the Roman Empire, marked by many changes. "A new era begins," a Roman citizen conversed with others in the forum.

Vita et regno Tiberii finitis, in historia Romana magni momenti intravit. "Tiberius in historia nostra manebit," magister in schola Romana dixit.

With the end of Tiberius's life and reign, he entered Roman history as a figure of great importance. "Tiberius will remain in our history," a teacher said in a Roman school.

In hoc capitulo, narratur finis regni Tiberii, mortis eius effectus in Roma et imperio, et eius hereditas historica. Mors Tiberii finem longi et complexi regni significat, quod multas res publicas Romanas affecit et in memoria populi variabiliter manet.

This chapter tells of the end of Tiberius's reign, the impact of his death on Rome and the empire, and his historical legacy. The death of Tiberius marked the end of a long and complex reign, which affected many aspects of Roman public affairs and remains variably remembered by the people.

Nero

Capitulum Primum: Incendium Magnum Romae

Anno sexagesimo quarto post Christum natum, magnum incendium Romae inopinate coepit. "Incendium in urbe est!" clamavit vigil urbis.

In the year 64 AD, a great fire unexpectedly started in Rome. "There is a fire in the city!" shouted the city watchman.

Ignis diu et vehementer per urbem arsit, domos et aedes consumens. "Ignis totam urbem consumit!" Romanus in via exclamavit.

The fire burned for a long time and fiercely through the city, consuming houses and buildings. "The fire is consuming the whole city!" a Roman exclaimed in the street.

Multae domus et templa, opes urbis, flammis deletae sunt. "Domus nostra ardet!" femina Romana, lacrimans, dixit.

Many houses and temples, the wealth of the city, were destroyed by the flames. "Our house is burning!" a Roman woman said, crying.

Populus Romanus, incendio viso, territus et confusus erat. "Quid faciemus?" puer in via territus rogavit.

The Roman people, seeing the fire, were terrified and confused. "What will we do?" a frightened boy asked in the street.

Nero, imperator Romanorum, in Antio erat cum nuntium de incendio accepit. "Roma ardet?" Nero, stupefactus, nuntio dixit.

Nero, the emperor of the Romans, was in Antium when he received news of the fire. "Is Rome burning?" Nero, stunned, said to the messenger.

Nero, incendium visurus, Romam celeriter rediit. "Romam redeo," Nero in curru suo dixit.

Nero, wanting to see the fire, quickly returned to Rome. "I am returning to Rome," Nero said in his chariot.

Rumores per urbem diffusi sunt, incendium a Nerone ipso factum esse. "Dicunt Neronem incendium fecisse," senator Romanus collegae suo susurravit.

Rumors spread throughout the city that the fire was started by Nero himself. "They say Nero started the fire," a Roman senator whispered to his colleague.

Nero, criminationes audiens, incendium negavit et Christianos pro incendio accusavit. "Christianos incendium fecisse dico," Nero in concilio dixit.

Nero, hearing the accusations, denied starting the fire and blamed the Christians for it. "I say the Christians started the fire," Nero said in council.

Christiani, a Nerone accusati, ad mortem damnati sunt, crudeliter puniti. "Christiani punientur," praeco in foro clamavit.

The Christians, accused by Nero, were condemned to death and cruelly punished. "The Christians will be punished," a herald shouted in the forum.

Nero, dum Roma ardebat, in hortis suis cantavit et citharam sonuit, ludibrio habens. "Nero cantat, dum Roma ardet," civis indignatus narravit.

While Rome burned, Nero sang and played the lyre in his gardens, mocking the situation. "Nero sings while Rome burns," an outraged citizen said.

Populus Romanus, Neronis actis visis, de eius sanitate et mente dubitavit. "Num Nero sanus est?" Romanus in taberna rogavit.

The Roman people, seeing Nero's actions, doubted his sanity and mind. "Is Nero sane?" a Roman asked in a tavern.

Incendium urbis septem dies integras duravit, magnam partem Romae destruens. "Septem dies iam ardet," matrona Romana dixit.

The city's fire lasted seven whole days, destroying a large part of Rome. "It has been burning for seven days now," a Roman matron said.

Post incendium, Nero magnos consilios de reaedificatione urbis cepit. "Urbem reaedificabimus," Nero architectis suis imperavit.

After the fire, Nero made great plans for rebuilding the city. "We will rebuild the city," Nero commanded his architects.

Nero Domum Auream, palatium splendidum et magnificum, exstruxit. "Domus Aurea erit mea," Nero, laetus, in palatio suo dixit.

Nero built the Domus Aurea, a splendid and magnificent palace. "The Domus Aurea will be mine," Nero said happily in his palace.

Incendium Magnum Romae eventus magni momenti in historia Romana manet, memoria populi semper inhaerens. "Incendium numquam obliviscemur," senex Romanus ad nepotem suum narravit.

The Great Fire of Rome remains a significant event in Roman history, always lingering in the people's memory. "We will never forget the fire," an old Roman told his grandson.

In hoc capitulo, narratur de magno incendio quod Romam anno 64 AD vastavit, effectus eius in urbem et populum Romanum, et de actionibus et responsionibus Neronis, imperatoris Romani. Incendium non solum urbis partem destruxit, sed etiam fundamenta mutavit quomodo populus Romanus imperatorem suum vidit et de Christianis cogitavit.

This chapter tells of the great fire that devastated Rome in 64 AD, its effects on the city and the Roman people, and the actions and responses of Nero, the Roman emperor. The fire not only destroyed part of the city, but it also changed the way the Roman people viewed their emperor and thought about the Christians.

Capitulum Secundum: Neronis Tyrannis

Nero imperium Romanum cum crudelitate et luxuria tenebat. "Imperabo ut volo," Nero in palatio suo dixit.

Nero held the Roman Empire with cruelty and luxury. "I will rule as I wish," Nero said in his palace.

Senatus Romanus timore Neronis replebatur. "Neronem timemus," senator Romanus alteri senatori susurravit.

The Roman Senate was filled with fear of Nero. "We fear Nero," a Roman senator whispered to another senator.

Nero spectacula grandia et ludi magnifici in circo et theatro dedit. "Ludos magnos populo do," Nero ad consiliarium suum dixit.

Nero gave grand spectacles and magnificent games in the circus and theater. "I give great games to the people," Nero said to his advisor.

Populus Romanus, licet gravatus, Neronis imperium sustinebat. "Neronis imperium ferre debemus," civis Romanus in foro cum amico colloquebatur.

The Roman people, though burdened, endured Nero's reign. "We must bear Nero's rule," a Roman citizen said while conversing with a friend in the forum.

Nero matrem suam, Agrippinam, necare iussit. "Mater mihi periculum est," Nero ad consiliarios suos dixit.

Nero ordered the death of his mother, Agrippina. "My mother is a danger to me," Nero said to his advisors.

Nero uxorem suam Octaviam repudiavit et Poppaeam Sabinam duxit. "Octaviam repudio, Poppaeam duco," Nero in concilio pronuntiavit.

Nero divorced his wife Octavia and married Poppaea Sabina. "I divorce Octavia, I marry Poppaea," Nero declared in council.

Luxuria Neronis et actus immorales noti erant et publice criticebantur. "Neronis luxuria excessiva est," Romanus in taberna dixit.

Nero's luxury and immoral acts were well-known and publicly criticized. "Nero's luxury is excessive," a Roman said in a tavern.

Seneca, philosophus et magister Neronis, a Nerone ad mortem coactus est. "Moriar," Seneca, tristis, sibi inquit.

Seneca, the philosopher and Nero's teacher, was forced to die by Nero. "I will die," Seneca said sadly to himself.

Nero artes amavit, in musicis et theatris saepe apparuit, sed imperium male administravit. "Artem amo, sed imperium difficile est," Nero, confusus, dixit.

Nero loved the arts, often appearing in musical performances and theater, but he mismanaged the empire. "I love art, but ruling is difficult," Nero said, confused.

Imperium Neronis corruptum et sine frenis erat, luxuria et crudelitate plenum. "Neronis imperium corruptum est," senator, sollicitus, in senatu dixit.

Nero's empire was corrupt and uncontrolled, full of luxury and cruelty. "Nero's empire is corrupt," a concerned senator said in the Senate.

Populus et senatus Romanus de mutatione imperii cogitabant, Neronis regno fatigati. "Mutatio necessaria est," civis Romanus in via dixit.

The Roman people and Senate thought about changing the empire, weary of Nero's reign. "Change is necessary," a Roman citizen said in the street.

Coniurationes contra Neronem in urbe creverunt, multos ad conspirationem incitantes. "Neronem deponere debemus," coniurator in secreto loco dixit.

Conspiracies against Nero grew in the city, encouraging many to join the plot. "We must depose Nero," a conspirator said in a secret place.

Nero, coniurationum conscius, suspectus et paranoicus factus est. "Coniurationes ubique sunt," Nero, timens, in palatio suo cogitabat.

Nero, aware of the conspiracies, became suspicious and paranoid. "There are conspiracies everywhere," Nero thought in fear in his palace.

Nero multos senatores et nobiles Romae necavit, suspicionibus ductus. "Senatores periculosos necabo," Nero, iratus, imperavit.

Nero killed many senators and nobles in Rome, driven by suspicions. "I will kill the dangerous senators," Nero ordered angrily.

Neronis tyrannis in historia Romana ut tempus infame et violentum manet. "Neronis tempus infamis in historia manebit," historiographus Romanus in libro suo scripsit.

Nero's tyranny remains in Roman history as an infamous and violent time. "Nero's infamous time will remain in history," a Roman historian wrote in his book.

In hoc capitulo, narratur de tyrannide Neronis, eius luxuria, crudelitate, et mala administratione imperii. Nero matrem suam necavit, uxorem repudiavit, et multis atrocitatibus indulgens, populum Romanum et senatum graviter afflixit. Coniurationes

*contra eum creverunt, et eius imperium ut tempus violentum et
corruptum in historia Romana recordatur.*

This chapter tells of Nero's tyranny, his luxury, cruelty, and poor
administration of the empire. Nero killed his mother, divorced his
wife, and indulged in many atrocities, severely afflicting the
Roman people and Senate. Conspiracies against him grew, and his
reign is remembered as a violent and corrupt time in Roman
history.

Capitulum Tertium: Coniuratio Pisonis

*Anno sexagesimo quinto post Christum natum, coniuratio
contra Neronem imperatorem facta est. "Coniuratio incipit," Piso
in secreto loco dixit.*

In the year 65 AD, a conspiracy against Emperor Nero was
formed. "The conspiracy begins," Piso said in a secret place.

*Gaius Calpurnius Piso, senator nobilis, coniurationem
adversus Neronem duxit. "Neronem deponere debemus," Piso aliis
senatoribus dixit.*

Gaius Calpurnius Piso, a noble senator, led the conspiracy
against Nero. "We must depose Nero," Piso said to the other
senators.

*Coniuratio secreta inter senatores et nonnullos milites facta est.
"Secretum servare debemus," senator coniuratus militi dixit.*

A secret conspiracy was formed between senators and some
soldiers. "We must keep the secret," a conspiring senator said to a
soldier.

*Senatores, Neronis tyrannidem finire cupientes, coniurationem
paraverunt. "Tyrannidem Neronis finire oportet," senator in
coniuratione locutus est.*

The senators, desiring to end Nero's tyranny, prepared the
conspiracy. "Nero's tyranny must end," a senator spoke during the
conspiracy.

Nuntii de coniuratione ad Neronem pervenerunt. "Coniuratio contra te est," nuntius Neroni in palatio dixit.

News of the conspiracy reached Nero. "There is a conspiracy against you," a messenger told Nero in the palace.

Nero, audita coniuratione, iratus et territus respondit. "Coniuratores puniam," Nero, iratus, dixit.

Nero, having heard of the conspiracy, responded angrily and fearfully. "I will punish the conspirators," Nero said angrily.

Multi coniurati a Nerone capti sunt et deinde necati. "Coniuratos capimus," praefectus praetorio Neroni nuntiavit.

Many conspirators were captured by Nero and then killed. "We have captured the conspirators," the praetorian prefect reported to Nero.

Piso et alii senatores, coniuratione detecta, mortem sibi consciverunt. "Moriar potius quam capiar," Piso, desperatus, sibi inquit.

Piso and other senators, with the conspiracy uncovered, took their own lives. "I will die rather than be captured," Piso said to himself in despair.

Coniuratio in urbe Romae magnam turbationem fecit. "Quid in urbe accidit?" civis Romanus in foro rogavit.

The conspiracy caused great turmoil in the city of Rome. "What is happening in the city?" a Roman citizen asked in the forum.

Post coniurationem, Nero in populo magis suspectus factus est. "Nero nos omnes suspectat," Romanus in via cum amico suo dixit.

After the conspiracy, Nero became more suspicious of the people. "Nero suspects us all," a Roman said to his friend on the street.

Nero, ad securitatem suam servandam, delatores et custodes adhibuit. "Delatores et custodes mihi necessarii sunt," Nero, timens, dixit.

Nero employed informers and guards to protect his security. "Informers and guards are necessary for me," Nero said, fearful.

Populus Romanus, rerum gestarum conscius, de imperii futuri sollicitus erat. "Quid futurum est?" matrona Romana in domo sua dixit.

The Roman people, aware of the events, were anxious about the future of the empire. "What will happen?" a Roman matron said in her home.

Senatus Romanus, Neronis potestatem et crudelitatem metuens, timebat. "Quid Nero faciet?" senator alteri senatori in curia susurravit.

The Roman Senate, fearing Nero's power and cruelty, was afraid. "What will Nero do?" a senator whispered to another senator in the Senate house.

Nero, post coniurationem, crudelior et suspectior factus est. "Crudelem me esse oportet," Nero, in palatio suo meditatus est.

After the conspiracy, Nero became more cruel and suspicious. "I must be cruel," Nero meditated in his palace.

Coniuratio Pisonis in historia Romana ut signum mutationis et tyrannidis Neronis manet. "Coniuratio Pisonis memoria nostra manebit," historiographus Romanus in libro suo scripsit.

The Piso conspiracy remains in Roman history as a symbol of change and Nero's tyranny. "The Piso conspiracy will remain in our memory," a Roman historian wrote in his book.

In hoc capitulo, coniuratio Pisonis contra Neronem et eius consequentiae in urbe Romana et in imperio descriptae sunt. Coniuratio magnam turbationem fecit et Nero, timore motus, crudelior factus est, quae mutationem in imperio significavit.

In this chapter, the Piso conspiracy against Nero and its consequences in the city of Rome and the empire are described. The conspiracy caused great turmoil, and Nero, driven by fear, became more cruel, marking a change in the empire.

Capitulum Quartum: Annus Quattuor Imperatorum

Anno sexagesimo octavo post Christum natum, Nero a senatu hostis publicus declaratus est. "Nero hostis publicus est," princeps senator in senatu exclamavit.

In the year 68 AD, Nero was declared a public enemy by the Senate. "Nero is a public enemy," the chief senator exclaimed in the Senate.

Galba, Otho, Vitellius, et Vespasianus, uno anno, imperatores Romani facti sunt. "Quattuor imperatores uno anno!" civis Romanus in foro stupens dixit.

Galba, Otho, Vitellius, and Vespasian became Roman emperors in a single year. "Four emperors in one year!" a Roman citizen said in astonishment in the forum.

Nero, senatus decreto territus, fugere conatus est, sed mox captus est. "Fugere non possum," Nero, desperatus, inquit.

Nero, terrified by the Senate's decree, tried to flee, but was soon captured. "I cannot escape," Nero said in despair.

Nero, captus et desperans, mortem sibi conscivit. "Moriendum est," Nero, tristis, sibi dixit.

Captured and in despair, Nero took his own life. "I must die," Nero said sadly to himself.

Galba, post Neronis mortem, primo imperator Romanorum factus est. "Galba imperator est," nuntius per urbem cucurrit.

After Nero's death, Galba was the first to become emperor of the Romans. "Galba is emperor," a messenger ran through the city announcing.

Otho, Galbae adversus, contra eum rebellavit et mox imperator ipse factus est. "Otho nunc imperat," praeco in Roma clamavit.

Otho, opposed to Galba, rebelled against him and soon became emperor himself. "Otho now rules," a herald shouted in Rome.

Vitellius, ab exercitu Germanico in Germania, imperator proclamatus est. "Vitellius imperator a militibus factus est," legatus Germanicus nuntiavit.

Vitellius was proclaimed emperor by the German army in Germany. "Vitellius has been made emperor by the soldiers," a German legate announced.

Otho et Vitellius de imperio pugnaverunt, gravi proelio commisso. "Otho et Vitellius pugnant," spectator in campo proelii dixit.

Otho and Vitellius fought for the empire, engaging in a fierce battle. "Otho and Vitellius are fighting," a spectator said on the battlefield.

Otho, proelio victus, mortem sibi conscivit, imperii spe perdita. "Otho se necavit," nuntius ad senatum rettulit.

Otho, defeated in battle, took his own life, having lost hope for the empire. "Otho has killed himself," a messenger reported to the Senate.

Vitellius, a senatu Romano imperator confirmatus est, post Othonis mortem. "Vitellius nunc Romae imperat," senator Romanus ad collegam suum dixit.

Vitellius was confirmed as emperor by the Roman Senate after Otho's death. "Vitellius now rules in Rome," a Roman senator said to his colleague.

Vespasianus, in oriente cum exercitu, imperium cepit, contra Vitellium movens. "Vespasianus venit," nuntius in castris militum dixit.

Vespasian, in the east with his army, took power and moved against Vitellius. "Vespasian is coming," a messenger said in the military camp.

Vespasianus Romam venit et ab exercitu et senatu imperator declaratus est. "Vespasianus nunc imperat," vox in foro sonuit.

Vespasian came to Rome and was declared emperor by both the army and the Senate. "Vespasian now rules," a voice sounded in the forum.

Annus quattuor imperatorum tumultu, bello, et mutationibus plenus erat. "Quattuor imperatores in uno anno!" historiographus in annalibus scripsit.

The Year of the Four Emperors was full of turmoil, war, and changes. "Four emperors in one year!" a historian wrote in the annals.

Vespasianus, post multas turbationes, imperium Romanum stabilivit. "Pax et ordo rediit," Vespasianus in senatu dixit.

Vespasian, after much turmoil, stabilized the Roman Empire. "Peace and order have returned," Vespasian said in the Senate.

Annus sexagesimus nonus post Christum natum finem Neronis tyrannidis et novi principii in imperio Romano significavit. "Nova aetas in imperio coepit," civis Romanus in via cum amico suo colloquebatur.

The year 69 AD marked the end of Nero's tyranny and the beginning of a new era in the Roman Empire. "A new age has begun in the empire," a Roman citizen said while conversing with his friend on the street.

In hoc capitulo, narratur tumultuosus annus 69 AD, qui "Annus Quattuor Imperatorum" nominatus est. Hoc anno, Nero mortem sibi conscivit, et Galba, Otho, Vitellius, et Vespasianus, uno anno, imperatores facti sunt. Hoc tempus magnae instabilitatis et mutationis in imperio Romano fuit, quod finem Neronis tyrannidis et novum principium sub Vespasiano significavit.

In this chapter, the tumultuous year 69 AD, known as the "Year of the Four Emperors," is described. During this year, Nero took his own life, and Galba, Otho, Vitellius, and Vespasian became emperors in the same year. This time was one of great instability and change in the Roman Empire, marking the end of Nero's tyranny and the beginning of a new era under Vespasian.

Capitulum Quintum: Neronis Hereditas

Nero, post mortem, in memoria Romana ut tyrannus infamis et artifex singularis manet. "Nero tyrannus et artifex fuit," magister in schola Romana discipulis suis narravit.

Nero, after his death, remains in Roman memory as a notorious tyrant and a unique artist. "Nero was both a tyrant and an artist," a teacher told his students in a Roman school.

Regnum Neronis pro luxuria et crudelitate notum est. "Neronis regnum luxuriosum et crudele erat," senex Romanus ad nepotem suum dixit.

Nero's reign is known for its luxury and cruelty. "Nero's reign was luxurious and cruel," an old Roman said to his grandson.

Domus Aurea, quam Nero aedificavit, eius opulentiam et vanitatem demonstrat. "Domus Aurea Neronis vanitatem ostendit," turista in ruinis palatii dixit.

The Domus Aurea, which Nero built, demonstrates his opulence and vanity. "The Domus Aurea shows Nero's vanity," a tourist said in the palace ruins.

Persecutio Christianorum sub Nerone tristis memoria in historia Romana est. "Christiani sub Nerone multa passi sunt," sacerdos in ecclesia Romana dixit.

The persecution of Christians under Nero is a sad memory in Roman history. "The Christians suffered greatly under Nero," a priest said in a Roman church.

Nero, artibus delectatus, musicam et theatrum amavit, sed male regnavit. "Nero artes amavit, sed male imperavit," poeta Romanus in colloquio dixit.

Nero, delighted by the arts, loved music and theater, but ruled poorly. "Nero loved the arts, but ruled poorly," a Roman poet said in conversation.

Mors Neronis mutationem significativam in imperio Romano adferebat. "Neronis mors imperii mutationem incipit," historiographus in academia dixit.

Nero's death brought about a significant change in the Roman Empire. "Nero's death marks the beginning of the empire's change," a historian said in the academy.

Post Neronem, imperium Romanum in novam aetatem ingressum est, magis stabilitatem quaerens. "Nova aetas post Neronem coepit," senator Romanus in curia loquebatur.

After Nero, the Roman Empire entered a new era, seeking greater stability. "A new age began after Nero," a Roman senator said in the Senate.

Historici de persona et regno Neronis multum disputant, eius gesta ponderantes. "Neronis regnum adhuc disputatur," professor in universitate Romana dixit.

Historians often debate the character and reign of Nero, weighing his deeds. "Nero's reign is still debated," a professor said at the Roman university.

Nero in litteris Romanis et in artibus saepe repraesentatus est, figura controversa. "Nero in litteris nostris apparet," scriptor in officina sua dixit.

Nero is often represented in Roman literature and the arts as a controversial figure. "Nero appears in our literature," a writer said in his workshop.

Incendium Romae sub Nerone factum inter fabulam et historiam versatur. "Neronis incendium inter veritatem et fabulam est," civis in bibliotheca Romana dixit.

The fire of Rome under Nero lies somewhere between myth and history. "Nero's fire is between truth and legend," a citizen said in the Roman library.

Imperium Romanum post Neronem stabilis factum est, eius tumultuosis temporibus finitis. "Post Neronem, pax in imperio fuit," magistratus in foro Romano dixit.

The Roman Empire became stable after Nero, with the end of his tumultuous times. "After Nero, there was peace in the empire," a magistrate said in the Roman forum.

Nero, exemplum tyranni Romani, in historia ut figura negativa manet. "Nero exemplum tyranni est," iuvenis in ludo Romano discit.

Nero, as an example of a Roman tyrant, remains a negative figure in history. "Nero is an example of a tyrant," a young student learned in a Roman school.

Domus Aurea Neronis, post eius mortem, destructa et obliterata est. "Domus Aurea nunc ruinis est," architectus in loco aedificii dixit.

Nero's Domus Aurea, after his death, was destroyed and obliterated. "The Domus Aurea is now in ruins," an architect said at the building site.

Imperium Neronis in historiographia Romana adhuc controversum est, eius acta ponderantes. "Neronis imperium adhuc in dubio est," scholaris in studiis suis dixit.

Nero's reign remains controversial in Roman historiography, as his deeds are weighed. "Nero's empire is still in question," a scholar said in his studies.

Nero, figura complexa et multiformis, in annalibus Romanis permansit, semper in memoria populi. "Nero in historia nostra manet," civis Romanus in colloquio cum amico suo dixit.

Nero, a complex and multifaceted figure, remained in the Roman annals, always in the people's memory. "Nero remains in our history," a Roman citizen said in conversation with his friend.

In hoc capitulo, hereditas Neronis imperatoris Romani exploratur, cum eius tyrannide, artibus, et impactu in historiam Romanam. Nero, post mortem, ut figura complexa et controversa in memoria Romana permansit, eius regnum et acta in litteris, artibus, et historiographia Romana repraesentata.

In this chapter, the legacy of the Roman emperor Nero is explored, including his tyranny, his love of the arts, and his impact on Roman history. After his death, Nero remained a complex and controversial figure in Roman memory, with his reign and actions represented in literature, the arts, and Roman historiography.

A Nero ad Vespasianum

Capitulum Primum: Nero et Eius Exitus

Nero, Romanorum imperator, populi favorem amittit. "Populus me non amat," Nero in palatio suo dixit.

Nero, the emperor of the Romans, loses the favor of the people. "The people do not love me," Nero said in his palace.

Senatus Romanus Neronem hostem publicum declarat. "Nero hostis publicus est," princeps senator in senatu exclamavit.

The Roman Senate declares Nero a public enemy. "Nero is a public enemy," the chief senator exclaimed in the Senate.

Territus senatus decreto, Nero Romam fugere conatur. "Fugere debeo," Nero, timens, cogitavit.

Terrified by the Senate's decree, Nero tries to flee Rome. "I must flee," Nero thought, afraid.

In fuga, Nero adiutores desperatim quaerit. "Quis me adiuvabit?" Nero, fugiens, rogavit.

In flight, Nero desperately seeks allies. "Who will help me?" Nero asked while fleeing.

Cum nullo auxilio invento, Nero mortem sibi consciscit. "Moriendum est," Nero, desperatus, inquit.

With no help found, Nero takes his own life. "I must die," Nero said in despair.

Neronis mors finem dynastiae Iuliae-Claudiae significat. "Dynastia Julia-Claudia finita est," historiographus Romanus postea scripsit.

Nero's death marks the end of the Julio-Claudian dynasty. "The Julio-Claudian dynasty is over," a Roman historian later wrote.

Populus Romanus Neronis mortem varie accipit. "Nero mortuus est," civis in foro ad alium dixit.

The Roman people receive the news of Nero's death with mixed feelings. "Nero is dead," a citizen said to another in the forum.

Rumores de Neronis fine celeriter per urbem diffunduntur. "Audistisne de Nerone?" inquisitor in via populo rogavit.

Rumors about Nero's end spread quickly throughout the city. "Have you heard about Nero?" a questioner asked the people in the street.

Galba, legatus in Hispania, imperator a militibus declaratur. "Galba imperator factus est," nuntius per provincias cucurrit.

Galba, a legate in Spain, is declared emperor by the soldiers. "Galba has been made emperor," a messenger ran through the provinces announcing.

Galba, audita Neronis morte, Romam ingreditur et imperium sibi vindicat. "Romam ingredior," Galba, iter faciens, dixit.

Galba, having heard of Nero's death, enters Rome and claims the empire for himself. "I am entering Rome," Galba said while traveling.

Initium regni Galbae turbidum et difficile est. "Difficile est imperare," Galba in curia loquitur.

The beginning of Galba's reign is turbulent and difficult. "It is difficult to rule," Galba said in the Senate.

Galba novas leges et reformas promittit, sed difficultates habet. "Reformas faciam," Galba in concilio dixit.

Galba promises new laws and reforms, but faces difficulties. "I will make reforms," Galba said in council.

Senatus Romanus, Neronis tyrannide liberatus, Galbam imperatorem suscipit. "Galbam suscipimus," senator in senatu pronuntiavit.

The Roman Senate, freed from Nero's tyranny, accepts Galba as emperor. "We accept Galba," a senator declared in the Senate.

Pars militum Galbam imperatorem non approbat, discordiam sentiens. "Galbam non volumus," miles in castris dixit.

A part of the soldiers does not approve of Galba as emperor, sensing discord. "We don't want Galba," a soldier said in the camp.

Regnum Galbae brevi tempore instabile est, multas difficultates habens. "Galbae imperium instabile est," civis Romanus in foro cum amico colloquebatur.

Galba's reign is unstable within a short time, facing many difficulties. "Galba's rule is unstable," a Roman citizen said while talking with a friend in the forum.

In hoc capitulo, exitus Neronis, ultimi imperatoris dynastiae Iuliae-Claudiae, et ascensus Galbae ad imperium narratur. Nero, populi favorem amisso et senatus hostem publicum declarato, fugit et mortem sibi consciscit. Galba, ut novus imperator, promittit reformas et leges novas, sed initium regni eius turbidum est, cum militum parte eum non approbante. Hoc tempus significat magnum mutationem in imperio Romano.

In this chapter, the end of Nero, the last emperor of the Julio-Claudian dynasty, and the rise of Galba to power is narrated. Nero, having lost the favor of the people and declared a public enemy by the Senate, flees and takes his own life. Galba, as the new emperor, promises reforms and new laws, but his reign begins in turmoil, with some soldiers not approving of him. This period marks a significant change in the Roman Empire.

Capitulum Secundum: Otho Contra Galbam

Otho, quondam amicus Galbae, contra eum secreta consilia capit. "Galbam superabo," Otho in secreto loco cogitavit.

Otho, once a friend of Galba, takes secret plans against him. "I will surpass Galba," Otho thought in a secret place.

Otho militibus magnas promissiones facit, ut eorum fidelitatem vincat. "Vobis multa promitto," Otho ad milites dixit.

Otho makes great promises to the soldiers in order to win their loyalty. "I promise you many things," Otho said to the soldiers.

Galba, Othonis proditione cognita, magnopere sollicitatur. "Otho me tradit!" Galba in palatio suo exclamavit.

Galba, having learned of Otho's betrayal, becomes greatly worried. "Otho betrays me!" Galba exclaimed in his palace.

Otho, militum auxilio innixus, imperium Romanum sibi vindicare conatur. "Imperium capiam," Otho confidenter affirmavit.

Otho, relying on the support of the soldiers, attempts to claim the Roman Empire for himself. "I will take the empire," Otho confidently declared.

Inter Othonis et Galbae copias conflictus est, urbis Romae vias sanguine tingentes. "Pugnate pro me!" Otho ad suos milites imperavit.

A conflict breaks out between Otho's and Galba's forces, staining the streets of Rome with blood. "Fight for me!" Otho ordered his soldiers.

Galba, in foro Romano, ab Othonis militibus crudeliter necatur. "Galba mortuus est," miles, gladio cruento, inquit.

Galba is cruelly killed by Otho's soldiers in the Roman Forum. "Galba is dead," a soldier said, with a bloodied sword.

Otho, post Galbae mortem, imperator Romanorum a militibus declaratur. "Otho nunc imperat," praeco in foro clamavit.

After Galba's death, Otho is declared emperor of the Romans by the soldiers. "Otho now rules," a herald shouted in the forum.

Otho, imperii potestate adeptus, novas politicas et administrationes incipit. "Nova a me incipient," Otho in senatu promisit.

Otho, having gained imperial power, begins new policies and reforms. "New things will begin with me," Otho promised in the Senate.

Populus Romanus, de novo imperatore Othone, dubitat et ambiguus est. "Quis est Otho?" civis Romanus in via rogavit.

The Roman people are doubtful and uncertain about the new emperor Otho. "Who is Otho?" a Roman citizen asked in the street.

Otho, imperii potestatem tenens, coniurationes et dissensiones internas patitur. "Coniurationes me circumdant," Otho anxie dixit.

Otho, holding the power of the empire, suffers from conspiracies and internal dissension. "Conspiracies surround me," Otho said anxiously.

Senatus Romanus Othonem reluctanter ut imperatorem accipit, dissensione motus. "Othonem suscipimus," senator invitus in senatu dixit.

The Roman Senate reluctantly accepts Otho as emperor, moved by dissension. "We accept Otho," a senator said unwillingly in the Senate.

Vitellius, Germaniae legatus, imperium Romanum etiam sibi vindicat. "Et ego imperabo," Vitellius apud milites suos dixit.

Vitellius, a legate in Germany, also claims the Roman Empire for himself. "I will rule as well," Vitellius said to his soldiers.

Bellum civile inter Othonem et Vitellium, de imperio decertantes, incipit. "Bellum est," nuntius in urbe Romana cucurrit.

A civil war begins between Otho and Vitellius, fighting for the empire. "It is war," a messenger ran through the city of Rome.

Romani, de imperii futuro solliciti, de belli eventu anxii sunt. "Quid futurum est?" matrona Romana in domo sua rogavit.

The Romans, anxious about the future of the empire, are worried about the outcome of the war. "What will happen?" a Roman matron asked in her home.

Otho, ad bellum contra Vitellium paratus, copias suas instruit. "Contra Vitellium pugnabimus," Otho ad generales suos dixit.

Otho, prepared for war against Vitellius, organizes his forces. "We will fight against Vitellius," Otho said to his generals.

In hoc capitulo, Otho, Galbae olim amicus, contra eum consilia capit et imperium sibi vindicat. Post Galbae necem, Otho imperator declaratur, sed cito coniurationes et bellum civile cum Vitellio facit. Otho novas politicas incipit, sed populus Romanus et senatus de eius imperio ambigui sunt. Bellum inter Othonem et Vitellium de imperii Romani fato decernit.

In this chapter, Otho, once a friend of Galba, plots against him and claims the empire for himself. After Galba's death, Otho is declared emperor but soon faces conspiracies and civil war with Vitellius. Otho initiates new policies, but the Roman people and Senate are uncertain about his rule. The war between Otho and Vitellius will decide the fate of the Roman Empire.

Capitulum Tertium: Bellum Civile et Vitellius

Vitellius, dux legionum Germanicarum, Romam movere statuit. "Romam movebo," Vitellius in consilio militari dixit.

Vitellius, leader of the German legions, decided to march on Rome. "I will move on Rome," Vitellius said in a military council.

Vitellius copias per Germaniam et Galliam diligenter colligit. "Milites colligamus," Vitellius ad legatos suos imperavit.

Vitellius carefully gathered troops throughout Germany and Gaul. "Let us gather soldiers," Vitellius commanded his legates.

Otho et Vitellius prope Cremonam in acie concurrunt. "Ad Cremonam pugnabimus," Otho instruxit.

Otho and Vitellius clashed in battle near Cremona. "We will fight at Cremona," Otho ordered.

Gravis pugna inter Othonis et Vitellii copias fit, multis cadentibus. "Fortiter pugnate!" Vitellius ad milites suos clamavit.

A fierce battle occurred between Otho's and Vitellius's forces, with many falling. "Fight bravely!" Vitellius shouted to his soldiers.

Otho in pugna Cremonae graviter victus est, copias suas cedentes videns. "Victi sumus," Otho in campo proelii dixit.

Otho was heavily defeated in the battle of Cremona, seeing his forces retreat. "We are defeated," Otho said on the battlefield.

Post cladem, Otho mortem sibi consciscit, dignitate motus. "Mori potius quam capi malo," Otho sibi inquit.

After the defeat, Otho took his own life, moved by a sense of dignity. "I prefer death to capture," Otho said to himself.

Vitellius, Cremonae victoria laetus, Romam petit ut imperator agnoscatur. "Romam ibimus," Vitellius ad milites suos dixit.

Vitellius, pleased with his victory at Cremona, headed to Rome to be recognized as emperor. "We will go to Rome," Vitellius said to his soldiers.

Vitellius, Romam ingressus, a militibus et populis acclamatur. "Vitellius imperator!" populus in viis exclamavit.

Vitellius, having entered Rome, was acclaimed by the soldiers and the people. "Vitellius, emperor!" the crowd shouted in the streets.

Vitellius in urbe Roma imperator declaratur, cum magnis celebrationibus. "Vitellius nunc imperat," praeco in foro Romano nuntiavit.

Vitellius was declared emperor in the city of Rome, with great celebrations. "Vitellius now rules," a herald announced in the Roman forum.

Imperator factus, Vitellius luxuria et epulis magnis indulget. "Epulemur!" Vitellius in palatio suo iubet.

Having become emperor, Vitellius indulged in luxury and great feasts. "Let us feast!" Vitellius ordered in his palace.

Senatus Romanus, Vitellium reluctanter ut imperatorem agnoscit. "Vitellium agnoscimus," senator in curia Romana suspiravit.

The Roman Senate reluctantly acknowledged Vitellius as emperor. "We recognize Vitellius," a senator sighed in the Roman Senate.

Vitellius administrationem laxam et saepe inefficacem habet. "Vitellius non bene regit," senator alii senatori dixit.

Vitellius had a lax and often ineffective administration. "Vitellius does not rule well," one senator said to another.

Vespasianus, in oriente, contra Vitellium se opponit, imperium petens. "Vitellium superabimus," Vespasianus in consilio militari dixit.

Vespasian, in the east, opposed Vitellius, seeking the empire. "We will defeat Vitellius," Vespasian said in a military council.

Romani, de Vitellii imperio querentes, mutationem desiderant. "Quid de imperio?" civis Romanus in foro rogavit.

The Romans, complaining about Vitellius's rule, desired a change. "What about the empire?" a Roman citizen asked in the forum.

Sub Vitellio, bellum civile in imperio Romano rursus incenditur. "Bellum civile rursus est," nuntius in urbe divulgavit.

Under Vitellius, civil war was reignited in the Roman Empire. "There is civil war again," a messenger announced in the city.

In hoc capitulo, Vitellius, dux legionum Germanicarum, imperium Romanum sibi vindicat post victoriam contra Othonem apud Cremonam. Vitellius, Romae imperator declaratus, luxuria indulget, sed administrationem inefficacem habet. Vespasianus in oriente contra Vitellium movet, et bellum civile in imperio rursus accenditur. Populus Romanus de novo imperatore Vitellio et de futura imperii directione sollicitus est.

In this chapter, Vitellius, leader of the German legions, claims the Roman Empire for himself after his victory over Otho at Cremona. Vitellius, declared emperor in Rome, indulges in luxury but has an ineffective administration. Vespasian, in the east, moves against Vitellius, and civil war reignites in the empire. The Roman people are anxious about the new emperor Vitellius and the future direction of the empire.

Capitulum Quartum: Ascensus Vespasiani

Vespasianus, Iudaeae legatus, imperium Romanum sibi vindicare statuit. "Imperium capiam," Vespasianus in consilio dixit.

Vespasian, the legate of Judea, decided to claim the Roman Empire for himself. "I will take the empire," Vespasian said in council.

In Oriente, Vespasianus magnas copias congregat ad imperium petendum. "Copias congregemus," Vespasianus ad legatos suos imperavit.

In the East, Vespasian gathered large forces to pursue the empire. "Let us gather the troops," Vespasian commanded his legates.

Vespasianus Aegyptum et alias orientis partes celeriter obtinet. "Aegyptum obtinemus," Vespasianus in epistula ad senatum scripsit.

Vespasian quickly took control of Egypt and other parts of the East. "We have obtained Egypt," Vespasian wrote in a letter to the Senate.

Militum et populorum auxilio confisus, Vespasianus ad imperium ascendit. "Populus et milites me sequuntur," Vespasianus confidenter affirmavit.

Relying on the support of soldiers and people, Vespasian rose to power. "The people and soldiers follow me," Vespasian confidently declared.

Roma et Italia Vespasianum ut imperatorem suscipiunt. "Vespasianum accipimus," vox populi Romani in foro sonuit.

Rome and Italy accepted Vespasian as emperor. "We accept Vespasian," the voice of the Roman people rang out in the forum.

Vitellius, Vespasiani successu territus, ad defensionem parat. "Vespasianum resistere debeo," Vitellius anxius in palatio suo dixit.

Vitellius, terrified by Vespasian's success, prepared for defense. "I must resist Vespasian," Vitellius anxiously said in his palace.

Vespasianus legiones ad Italiam mittit ad imperium capiendum. "Legiones in Italiam mittamus," Vespasianus ad milites suos dixit.

Vespasian sent legions to Italy to capture the empire. "Let us send legions to Italy," Vespasian said to his soldiers.

Vitellius et Vespasianus ad ultimum conflictum in Italia se preparant. "Ad ultimum bellum parati sumus," Vespasianus inquit.

Vitellius and Vespasian prepared for their final conflict in Italy. "We are ready for the final battle," Vespasian said.

Vespasiani copiae Romam appropinquant, urbi et imperio minantes. "Romam appropinquamus," dux Vespasiani exercitus clamavit.

Vespasian's forces approached Rome, threatening the city and the empire. "We are approaching Rome," the commander of Vespasian's army shouted.

Vitellius, desperatione et metu afficitur, copiarum adventum audiens. "Quid faciam?" Vitellius, territus, in palatio suo meditabatur.

Vitellius, overwhelmed by desperation and fear, heard of the approaching forces. "What shall I do?" Vitellius, terrified, pondered in his palace.

Magnus conflictus inter Vitellium et Vespasianum in Italia geritur. "Pro Vespasiano pugnate!" centurio in acie clamavit.

A great conflict between Vitellius and Vespasian took place in Italy. "Fight for Vespasian!" a centurion shouted on the battlefield.

Vitellius, a suis militibus desertus, spem imperii amittit. "Desertus sum," Vitellius in desperatione dixit.

Vitellius, abandoned by his soldiers, lost hope for the empire. "I am deserted," Vitellius said in despair.

Vespasianus, Romae victoriam reportans, imperator salutatur. "Victoria nostra est," Vespasianus apud Portam Romanam exclamavit.

Vespasian, bringing victory to Rome, was hailed as emperor. "The victory is ours," Vespasian exclaimed at the Roman Gate.

Vespasianus in Roma imperator Romanorum sollemniter declaratur. "Vespasianus imperator est," praeco in foro Romano nuntiavit.

Vespasian was solemnly declared emperor of the Romans in Rome. "Vespasian is emperor," a herald announced in the Roman forum.

Post victoriam, Vespasianus reformationes et restaurationes in imperio incipit. "Reformare et restaurare incipiamus," Vespasianus in senatu Romano dixit.

After his victory, Vespasian began reforms and restorations in the empire. "Let us begin reforms and restoration," Vespasian said in the Roman Senate.

In hoc capitulo, narratur ascensus Vespasiani ad imperium Romanum. Vespasianus, Iudaeae legatus, copias in oriente congregat et Aegyptum obtinet. Cum supporto militum et populorum, Vespasianus Romam movet et Vitellius cum eo in Italia confligit. Vespasianus, victoria apud Romam reportata, imperator declaratur et reformationes in imperio incipit, novam aetatem in imperio Romano inaugurans.

In this chapter, the rise of Vespasian to the Roman Empire is narrated. Vespasian, the legate of Judea, gathers forces in the East and captures Egypt. With the support of soldiers and people, Vespasian moves toward Rome and clashes with Vitellius in Italy. After securing victory at Rome, Vespasian is declared emperor and begins reforms in the empire, inaugurating a new era in the Roman Empire.

Capitulum Quintum: Novum Principium sub Vespasiano

Vespasianus, imperium adeptus, pacem et stabilitatem in imperio quaerit. "Pacem stabilitatemque quaeramus," Vespasianus in consilio dixit.

Vespasian, having gained the empire, seeks peace and stability within the empire. "Let us seek peace and stability," Vespasian said in council.

Leges et ordines in imperio Romano Vespasianus restituit. "Leges ordinesque restituam," Vespasianus ad senatum dixit.

Vespasian restored laws and order in the Roman Empire. "I will restore laws and order," Vespasian said to the Senate.

Imperium Romanum Vespasianus reformat et fortificat, ad futurum praeparans. "Imperium reformabo et fortificabo," Vespasianus ad consiliarios suos affirmavit.

Vespasian reformed and strengthened the Roman Empire, preparing it for the future. "I will reform and fortify the empire," Vespasian assured his advisors.

Aedificationes publicas magnas Romae Vespasianus incipit. "Roma aedificetur," Vespasianus architectis imperavit.

Vespasian began major public buildings in Rome. "Let Rome be built," Vespasian ordered the architects.

In fiscalibus rebus, Vespasianus prudentiam et moderationem adhibet. "Fiscus prudenter administretur," Vespasianus ad quaestorem dixit.

In financial matters, Vespasian applied prudence and moderation. "Let the treasury be managed wisely," Vespasian told the quaestor.

Senatus Romanus Vespasianum laudat pro eius prudentia et virtute. "Vespasianum laudamus," senator in curia Romana exclamavit.

The Roman Senate praised Vespasian for his prudence and virtue. "We praise Vespasian," a senator exclaimed in the Roman Senate.

Fidem militum et populi Vespasianus habet, eius auctoritatem affirmans. "Militibus et populo fido," Vespasianus in oratione dixit.

Vespasian had the loyalty of the soldiers and the people, affirming his authority. "I trust the soldiers and the people," Vespasian said in his speech.

Provincias Romani imperii Vespasianus stabilizat, pacem et securitatem promovens. "Provincias stabilizemus," Vespasianus in edicto suo scripsit.

Vespasian stabilized the provinces of the Roman Empire, promoting peace and security. "Let us stabilize the provinces," Vespasian wrote in his edict.

Cultum imperatoris modestum Vespasianus tenet, humilitate nota. "Modeste imperabo," Vespasianus in vita quotidiana demonstravit.

Vespasian maintained a modest imperial lifestyle, known for his humility. "I will rule modestly," Vespasian demonstrated in his daily life.

Bellum in Iudaea Vespasianus perficit, pacem in regione restituens. "Iudaeam pacemus," Vespasianus in consilio militari dixit.

Vespasian completed the war in Judea, restoring peace in the region. "Let us pacify Judea," Vespasian said in the military council.

Artes et litteras Vespasianus fovet, culturam Romanam augens. "Artes litterasque foveamus," Vespasianus ad patronos artium dixit.

Vespasian encouraged the arts and literature, enhancing Roman culture. "Let us support the arts and literature," Vespasian said to the patrons of the arts.

Imperium diu et feliciter Vespasianus tenet, prosperitatem imperii augens. "Diuturna felicitas imperii sit," Vespasianus in oratione ad populum dixit.

Vespasian held the empire for a long and successful reign, increasing its prosperity. "Let the empire have lasting happiness," Vespasian said in a speech to the people.

Titum, filium suum, Vespasianus ut successorem designat. "Titus post me imperabit," Vespasianus ad Titum dixit.

Vespasian designated his son Titus as his successor. "Titus will rule after me," Vespasian said to Titus.

In historia Romana, Vespasianus ut princeps bonus et stabilis manet. "Vespasianus bonus imperator fuit," historiographus Romanus postea scripsit.

In Roman history, Vespasian remains a good and stable ruler. "Vespasian was a good emperor," a Roman historian later wrote.

Vespasianus novam aetatem in imperio Romano inaugurat, reformationibus et stabilitate. "Nova aetas incipit," civis Romanus in foro cum amico suo colloquebatur.

Vespasian inaugurated a new era in the Roman Empire, with reforms and stability. "A new age begins," a Roman citizen said in the forum while talking to a friend.

In hoc capitulo, Vespasianus, novus imperator Romanus, pacem et stabilitatem in imperio quaerit et leges ordinesque restituit. Aedificationes publicas incipit, fiscalibus rebus prudentiam adhibet, et fidem militum et populi habet. Vespasianus provincias stabilizat, cultum imperatoris modestum tenet, et artes et litteras fovet. Imperium diu et feliciter tenet, et Titum filium suum ut successorem designat, novam aetatem in imperio Romano inaugurans.

In this chapter, Vespasian, the new Roman emperor, seeks peace and stability in the empire and restores laws and order. He begins public buildings, applies prudence in financial matters, and gains the loyalty of soldiers and the people. Vespasian stabilizes the provinces, maintains a modest imperial lifestyle, and supports the arts and literature. He holds the empire for a long and successful reign and designates his son Titus as his successor, inaugurating a new era in the Roman Empire.

Romanorum in Britannia Historia

Capitulum Primum: Adventus Romanorum

Romani, sub Iulio Caesare, primum Britanniam attigerunt. "Britanniam attingamus," Caesar ad milites suos dixit.

The Romans, under Julius Caesar, first reached Britain. "Let us reach Britain," Caesar said to his soldiers.

Britannia, terra divisa et barbara, Romanis incognita erat. "Terra incognita est," explorator Romanus ad Caesarem rettulit.

Britain, a divided and barbaric land, was unknown to the Romans. "It is an unknown land," a Roman scout reported to Caesar.

Romani, terram explorare cupientes, cum Britannis primum conflictum habuerunt. "Pugnemus," dux Romanus in acie clamavit.

The Romans, desiring to explore the land, had their first conflict with the Britons. "Let us fight," a Roman commander shouted in the battle line.

Prima expeditione non plene successa, Romani ad suas terras redierunt. "Revertamur," Caesar post proelium dixit.

With the first expedition not fully successful, the Romans returned to their own lands. "Let us return," Caesar said after the battle.

Claudius, imperator Romanus, novam expeditionem in Britanniam paravit. "Britanniam iterum petamus," Claudius in senatu Romano pronuntiavit.

Claudius, the Roman emperor, prepared a new expedition to Britain. "Let us seek Britain again," Claudius proclaimed in the Roman Senate.

Aulus Plautius, dux peritus, a Claudio in Britanniam missus est. "Britanniam subigemus," Plautius ad legiones suas dixit.

Aulus Plautius, an experienced general, was sent to Britain by Claudius. "We will subdue Britain," Plautius said to his legions.

Romanorum legiones audacter flumen Thamesis transierunt. "Flumen transeamus," Plautius ad milites in ripa fluminis imperavit.

The Roman legions boldly crossed the River Thames. "Let us cross the river," Plautius ordered his soldiers on the riverbank.

Britanni, diversis regibus ducti, Romanis resistere conabantur. "Romanos repellamus," Caratacus, dux Britannorum, ad suos clamavit.

The Britons, led by various kings, tried to resist the Romans. "Let us repel the Romans," Caratacus, a British leader, shouted to his people.

Caratacus, dux Britannorum, Romanos fortiter et audacter oppugnavit. "Pro libertate pugnate," Caratacus in acie Britannorum duxit.

Caratacus, leader of the Britons, fought the Romans bravely and boldly. "Fight for freedom," Caratacus led in the British battle line.

Romani, licet adversis, multas victorias in Britannia reportaverunt. "Victoriam reportamus," centurio Romanus ad suos in castris nuntiavit.

The Romans, despite challenges, won many victories in Britain. "We have won a victory," a Roman centurion announced to his men in the camp.

Romanorum castra et vias per insulam aedificabant, potestatem firmantes. "Castra et vias aedificemus," ingenarius Romanus in campo instruxit.

The Romans built forts and roads throughout the island, strengthening their power. "Let us build forts and roads," a Roman engineer directed in the field.

Commercia inter Romanos et Britannos quosdam coepit. "Commercium cum Romanis habeamus," princeps Britannus ad populum suum dixit.

Trade began between some Romans and Britons. "Let us have trade with the Romans," a British chieftain said to his people.

Cultura Romana in Britannia paulatim diffundebatur, moribus Britannicis immixta. "Cultura Romana nos afficit," Britannus in vico suo colloquebatur.

Roman culture gradually spread in Britain, blending with British customs. "Roman culture is influencing us," a Briton said in his village.

Romanorum potestas in parte meridionali Britanniae sensim aucta est. "Romanorum potestas crescit," explorator Romanus ad Plautium rettulit.

The Romans' power gradually increased in the southern part of Britain. "Roman power is growing," a Roman scout reported to Plautius.

Britannia, post multas res gestas, paulatim sub Romanorum imperium venit. "Britannia nunc Romana est," Plautius, victor, ad Claudium imperatorem nuntiavit.

Britain, after many events, gradually came under Roman rule. "Britain is now Roman," Plautius, victorious, reported to Emperor Claudius.

In hoc capitulo, adventus Romanorum in Britanniam sub Iulio Caesare et Claudio imperatore narratur. Romani, terram explorantes et cum Britannis pugnantes, paulatim potestatem in insula auctam habent. Cum Carataco, duce Britannorum, pugnant, castra et vias aedificant, et culturam Romanam diffundunt. Britannia, post resistentiam et conflictum, sub imperium Romanum venit.

In this chapter, the arrival of the Romans in Britain under Julius Caesar and Emperor Claudius is described. The Romans, exploring the land and fighting the Britons, gradually increased their power on the island. They fought with Caratacus, leader of the Britons, built forts and roads, and spread Roman culture. After resistance and conflict, Britain came under Roman rule.

Capitulum Secundum: Rebellio Boudicae

Iceni, Britannorum gens, a Romanis graviter oppressi sunt. "Graviter opprimimur," dux Icenorum ad suos dixit.

The Iceni, a tribe of the Britons, were heavily oppressed by the Romans. "We are greatly oppressed," the leader of the Iceni said to his people.

Boudica, regina Icenorum, rebellionem magnam contra Romanos duxit. "Rebellionem incipiamus," Boudica ad populum suum clamavit.

Boudica, queen of the Iceni, led a great rebellion against the Romans. "Let us start a rebellion," Boudica shouted to her people.

Boudicae copiae Camulodunum, Romanorum coloniam, vehementer destruxerunt. "Camulodunum destruamus," Boudica in acie hortata est.

Boudica's forces fiercely destroyed Camulodunum, a Roman colony. "Let us destroy Camulodunum," Boudica urged in battle.

Romani, sub Gaius Suetonius Paulinus, ad rebellionem Boudicae respondendum parabant. "Respondeamus," Suetonius ad milites suos dixit.

The Romans, under Gaius Suetonius Paulinus, prepared to respond to Boudica's rebellion. "Let us respond," Suetonius said to his soldiers.

Boudica, cum copiis suis, Londinium et Verulamium cepit et vastavit. "Londinium capiamus," Boudica, urbem spectans, dixit.

Boudica, with her forces, captured and destroyed Londinium and Verulamium. "Let us capture Londinium," Boudica said, gazing at the city.

Suetonius, cum Romanorum legionibus, ad bellum cum Boudica celeriter properavit. "Ad bellum properemus," Suetonius ad legiones suas imperavit.

Suetonius, with the Roman legions, quickly hurried to war against Boudica. "Let us hurry to battle," Suetonius commanded his legions.

Dura pugna inter Romanos et copias Boudicae facta est. "Pro Imperio pugnate!" Suetonius ad Romanos in acie clamavit.

A fierce battle took place between the Romans and Boudica's forces. "Fight for the Empire!" Suetonius shouted to the Romans on the battlefield.

Romani, disciplina militari et tactica superiore, victoriam contra Boudicam reportaverunt. "Victoriam reportavimus," centurio Romanus post pugnam exclamavit.

The Romans, with superior military discipline and tactics, achieved victory against Boudica. "We have won the victory," a Roman centurion exclaimed after the battle.

Boudica, cladem acceptam, mortem sibi consciscit, ne caperetur. "Mori malo quam capi," Boudica, desperata, sibi inquit.

Boudica, after suffering defeat, took her own life to avoid capture. "I prefer to die rather than be captured," Boudica said to herself in despair.

Rebellio Boudicae magna clades et calamitas Britannorum fuit. "Magna clades accidit," Britannus post rebellionem dixit.

Boudica's rebellion was a great disaster and calamity for the Britons. "A great disaster has occurred," a Briton said after the rebellion.

Romani, rebellionem Boudicae compressam, in Britannia potestatem firmiter tenuerunt. "Britanniam retinemus," Suetonius ad senatum Romam nuntiavit.

The Romans, having suppressed Boudica's rebellion, firmly held their power in Britain. "We hold Britain," Suetonius reported to the Senate in Rome.

Pax Romanorum, post rebellionem, in Britannia restituta est. "Pax nunc est," praefectus Romanus in castris dixit.

The Roman peace was restored in Britain after the rebellion. "There is now peace," a Roman prefect said in the camp.

Auctoritas Romanorum in insula Britannia post rebellionem consolidata est. "Auctoritatem nostram firmavimus," legatus Romanus ad milites suos dixit.

Roman authority in the island of Britain was consolidated after the rebellion. "We have strengthened our authority," a Roman legate said to his soldiers.

Cultura et leges Romanae in Britannia post rebellionem magis radices egerunt. "Leges Romanas doceamus," magister Romanus in schola Britanniae dixit.

Roman culture and laws took deeper root in Britain after the rebellion. "Let us teach Roman laws," a Roman teacher said in a school in Britain.

Britannia, post rebellionem Boudicae, magis in imperium Romanum integrata est. "Nunc Britannia plene Romana est," civis Romanus in foro Londinii colloquebatur.

After Boudica's rebellion, Britain became more integrated into the Roman Empire. "Now Britain is fully Roman," a Roman citizen said while conversing in the forum of Londinium.

In hoc capitulo, narratur de rebellione Boudicae, reginae Icenorum, contra Romanos. Rebellio, quamquam initio valida, a Romanis sub Gaius Suetonius Paulinus compressa est. Boudica, post cladem, mortem sibi consciscit, et pax Romanorum in Britannia restituta est. Romanorum auctoritas in insula firmata est, et cultura Romana magis in Britannia diffundebatur.

In this chapter, the rebellion of Boudica, queen of the Iceni, against the Romans is recounted. The rebellion, though strong at first, was crushed by the Romans under Gaius Suetonius Paulinus. Boudica, after her defeat, took her own life, and Roman peace was restored in Britain. Roman authority was strengthened on the island, and Roman culture spread further in Britain.

Capitulum Tertium: Gnaeus Julius Agricola

Gnaeus Julius Agricola, gubernator Britanniae, a Roma nominatus est. "Agricolam Britanniae praeficimus," imperator Romanus in senatu dixit.

Gnaeus Julius Agricola, governor of Britain, was appointed by Rome. "We appoint Agricola as governor of Britain," the Roman emperor said in the Senate.

Agricola, dux peritus et audax, in Britanniam Septentrionalem expeditiones multas duxit. "Ad Septentriones movebimus," Agricola ad milites suos dixit.

Agricola, an experienced and bold leader, led many expeditions into Northern Britain. "We will move north," Agricola said to his soldiers.

Agricola tribus Britannicis resistentes fortiter subegit. "Subigamus tribus," Agricola in consilio militari imperavit.

Agricola bravely subdued the resisting British tribes. "Let us subdue the tribes," Agricola commanded in the military council.

Vias, castra, et oppida Romanorum in Britannia aedificavit. "Vias et castra aedificemus," Agricola ad architectos suos dixit.

He built Roman roads, forts, and towns in Britain. "Let us build roads and forts," Agricola said to his architects.

Agricola, cum exercitu, Romanorum potestatem in Caledoniam extendit. "Caledoniam adimamus," Agricola ad legiones suas hortatus est.

With his army, Agricola extended Roman power into Caledonia. "Let us take Caledonia," Agricola urged his legions.

Cultura Romana apud Britannos a Agricola promota est. "Culturam Romanam Britannis demus," Agricola in oratione ad populum Britannum dixit.

Roman culture was promoted among the Britons by Agricola. "Let us bring Roman culture to the Britons," Agricola said in a speech to the British people.

Leges Romanas et iustitiam in Britannia Agricola stabilivit. "Iustitiam et leges Romanas statuamus," Agricola in iudicio dixit.

Agricola established Roman laws and justice in Britain. "Let us establish Roman justice and laws," Agricola said in court.

Agricola, bellum et pacem in Britannia administrans, laude dignus erat. "Agricola est laudandus," senator Romanus in Roma dixit.

Agricola, managing both war and peace in Britain, was worthy of praise. "Agricola is to be praised," a Roman senator said in Rome.

Agricola, cum Romanis in Caledonia pugnans, a Tacito historico in annalibus descriptus est. "Agricolae gesta scribamus," Tacitus, historiographus, cogitavit.

Agricola, fighting with the Romans in Caledonia, was described in the annals by the historian Tacitus. "Let us write about Agricola's deeds," Tacitus, the historian, thought.

Agricola fines Romanorum in Britannia ad maximum extendit. "Fines nostros ampliemus," Agricola ad consiliarios suos dixit.

Agricola extended Roman borders in Britain to their furthest extent. "Let us expand our borders," Agricola said to his advisors.

Legiones Romanas disciplina et virtute instruxit. "Legiones fortes et disciplinatas habeamus," Agricola in castris militum dixit.

He trained the Roman legions in discipline and virtue. "Let us have strong and disciplined legions," Agricola said in the military camp.

Quidam Britannorum cum Romanis pacem fecerunt, Romanorum potestate accepta. "Pacem cum Romanis faciamus," princeps Britannus ad suos dixit.

Some Britons made peace with the Romans, accepting Roman rule. "Let us make peace with the Romans," a British chief said to his people.

Agricola, in Britannia regnans, Romanorum imperium in insula confirmavit. "Imperium nostrum confirmemus," Agricola in concilio dixit.

Agricola, governing in Britain, strengthened Roman control over the island. "Let us solidify our empire," Agricola said in council.

Cultura Britannica et Romana in insula coalescebant, inter se miscebantur. "Culturae nostrae miscentur," Romanus in Britannia colloquebatur.

British and Roman cultures began to merge on the island, mixing with each other. "Our cultures are blending," a Roman said in Britain.

Agricola, post annos multos in Britannia, Romam reversus est. "Romam redeo," Agricola, finito imperio, sibi inquit.

After many years in Britain, Agricola returned to Rome. "I return to Rome," Agricola said to himself, as his command ended.

In hoc capitulo, gesta Gnaei Iulii Agricolae, gubernatoris Britanniae, enarrantur. Agricola, peritus dux Romanus, expeditiones in Britanniam Septentrionalem duxit, tribus resistentes subegit, et culturam Romanam promovit. Agricola fines Romanorum in insula extendit et legiones Romanas disciplina et virtute instruxit. Sub eius imperio, cultura Romana et Britannica in insula mixtae sunt. Agricola, post annos in Britannia, ad Romam rediit, eius gesta in historia Romana notabilia relicto.

In this chapter, the deeds of Gnaeus Julius Agricola, governor of Britain, are recounted. Agricola, a skilled Roman leader, led expeditions into Northern Britain, subdued resisting tribes, and promoted Roman culture. Agricola extended Roman borders on the island and trained Roman legions in discipline and virtue. Under his rule, Roman and British cultures mixed on the island. After years in Britain, Agricola returned to Rome, leaving behind notable achievements in Roman history.

Capitulum Quartum: Conflictus et Pax

Romani et Britanni saepe in conflictu erant, territorium et potestatem contendentes. "Contra Britannos pugnemus," dux Romanus in castris suis dixit.

The Romans and Britons were often in conflict, contending for territory and power. "Let us fight against the Britons," the Roman commander said in his camp.

Legiones Romanae rebelliones Britannicas strenue et frequenter represserunt. "Rebellionem reprimamus," legatus Romanus ad milites suos imperavit.

The Roman legions vigorously and frequently suppressed British rebellions. "Let us suppress the rebellion," the Roman legate ordered his soldiers.

Interdum, pax in insula Britannia inter Romanos et Britannos stabilita est. "Pacem habeamus," praefectus Romanus in concilio cum Britannis dixit.

Sometimes, peace was established between the Romans and Britons on the island of Britain. "Let us have peace," the Roman prefect said in council with the Britons.

Commercia et cultura inter Romanos et Britannos sensim augebantur. "Commercia nostra cum Romanis crescunt," mercator Britannus ad collegam suum dixit.

Trade and culture between the Romans and Britons gradually increased. "Our trade with the Romans is growing," a British merchant said to his colleague.

Sub imperio Romano, Britannia partem provinciae Romanae efficit. "Britannia nunc pars Romana est," civis Romanus in foro Londinii dixit.

Under Roman rule, Britain became part of a Roman province. "Britain is now Roman," a Roman citizen said in the forum of Londinium.

Romanorum viae et urbes per Britanniam transierunt, insulam transformantes. "Vias et urbes aedificemus," ingenarius Romanus in Britannia laborans dixit.

Roman roads and cities spread across Britain, transforming the island. "Let us build roads and cities," a Roman engineer working in Britain said.

Romani multas balneas, theatra, et fora in Britannia aedificaverunt. "Balneas hic aedificamus," architectus Romanus in Britannia inquit.

The Romans built many baths, theaters, and forums in Britain. "We are building baths here," a Roman architect in Britain said.

Britanni, cultura Romana affecti, mores et consuetudines Romanas susceperunt. "Romanorum mores discamus," iuvenis Britannus ad amicum suum dixit.

The Britons, influenced by Roman culture, adopted Roman customs and traditions. "Let us learn Roman customs," a young Briton said to his friend.

Legiones Romanae in Britannia castra fortia et praesidia constituerunt. "Castra hic ponamus," centurio Romanus in loco strategico dixit.

The Roman legions established strong forts and garrisons in Britain. "Let us set up a camp here," a Roman centurion said at a strategic location.

Potestas Romanorum in Britannia interdum a Britannis resistebatur. "Romanos resistamus," dux Britannus ad suos in concilio dixit.

Roman power in Britain was at times resisted by the Britons. "Let us resist the Romans," a British leader said to his people in council.

Britanni, leges Romanas et culturam discendo, in societatem Romanam integrabantur. "Leges Romanas discamus," magister Britannus in schola dixit.

The Britons, learning Roman laws and culture, were integrated into Roman society. "Let us learn Roman laws," a British teacher said in school.

Culturae Romanorum et Britannorum in insula coalescebant, inter se miscebantur. "Culturae nostrae miscentur," Romanus in Britannia cum amico Britannico colloquebatur.

The cultures of the Romans and Britons were merging on the island, mixing with each other. "Our cultures are blending," a Roman in Britain said while talking to his British friend.

Sub Romanis, pax et prosperitas in Britannia sensim augebantur. "Pax et prosperitas nunc sunt," agricultor Britannus in agro suo dixit.

Under the Romans, peace and prosperity gradually increased in Britain. "There is now peace and prosperity," a British farmer said in his field.

Britannia, ut provincia Romana, ad imperium Romanum multa contribuebat. "Provincia nostra ad Imperium contribuit," administrator Romanus in Britannia dixit.

As a Roman province, Britain contributed much to the Roman Empire. "Our province contributes to the Empire," a Roman administrator in Britain said.

Societas inter Romanos et Britannos in historia longe manebat, effectus diuturnos habens. "Historia nostra cum Romanis longa est," senex Britannus ad nepotes suos narravit.

The relationship between the Romans and Britons lasted long in history, having lasting effects. "Our history with the Romans is long," an elderly Briton told his grandchildren.

In hoc capitulo, conflictus et pax inter Romanos et Britannos in insula Britannia enarrantur. Rebelliones a Romanis repressae sunt, et commercia, cultura, et mores inter duas culturas coalescunt. Pax interdum stabilitur, et Britannia, sub Romanorum imperio, prosperitatem et integrationem culturalem experitur. Societas inter Romanos et Britannos diu in historia manet, cum Britannia ad imperium Romanum multum contribuit.

In this chapter, the conflicts and peace between the Romans and Britons on the island of Britain are described. The Romans suppressed rebellions, and trade, culture, and customs between the two cultures merged. Peace was at times established, and Britain, under Roman rule, experienced prosperity and cultural integration. The relationship between the Romans and Britons remained long in history, with Britain contributing much to the Roman Empire.

Capitulum Quintum: Romanorum Exitus

Romani, post saecula dominii, a Britannia recedere coeperunt. "Britanniam relinquamus," dux Romanus in consilio militari dixit.

The Romans, after centuries of rule, began to withdraw from Britain. "Let us leave Britain," the Roman commander said in a military council.

Imperium Romanum, oppressionibus externis et internis laborans, debilitatur. "Imperium laborat," imperator Romanus in Roma sollicitus dixit.

The Roman Empire, struggling with external and internal pressures, became weakened. "The empire is struggling," the Roman emperor said anxiously in Rome.

Romani, Britanniam defendere non valentes, copias suas retraxerunt. "Non possumus defendere," legatus Romanus in Britannia dixit.

The Romans, unable to defend Britain, withdrew their forces. "We cannot defend it," the Roman legate in Britain said.

Britanni, Romanis recedentibus, ad defendendum se ipsos paraverunt. "Nos ipsos defendamus," dux Britannicus ad suos clamavit.

The Britons, as the Romans withdrew, prepared to defend themselves. "Let us defend ourselves," a British leader shouted to his people.

Tribus Britannicae, Romanorum absentia, potestatem in insula recuperaverunt. "Potestatem nostram recuperemus," princeps Britannus in concilio tribuum dixit.

The British tribes, with the absence of the Romans, regained power on the island. "Let us regain our power," a British chief said in the tribal council.

Legati Romani, cum copiis militum, Britanniam reliquerunt. "Britanniam relinquimus," legatus Romanus ad milites suos dixit.

The Roman legates, along with their military forces, left Britain. "We are leaving Britain," the Roman legate said to his soldiers.

Aedificia, viae, et urbes Romanorum in Britannia relictae sunt. "Reliquiae Romanae manent," explorator Britannicus in ruina urbis Romanae observavit.

The Roman buildings, roads, and cities were left behind in Britain. "Roman remains still exist," a British scout observed in the ruins of a Roman city.

Cultura Romana, in Britannia diu vigens, vestigia relinquit. "Vestigia Romana videmus," Britannus in villa Romana dixit.

Roman culture, long thriving in Britain, left its traces. "We see Roman traces," a Briton said in a Roman villa.

Britanni, Romanorum hereditatem tenentes, novam aetatem inceperunt. "Nova aetas incipit," sapiens Britannicus in concilio dixit.

The Britons, holding onto the Roman legacy, began a new era. "A new age begins," a wise Briton said in a council.

Romanorum occupatio in Britannia finita, aetatem obscuram in insula inchoavit. "Aetas obscura inchoatur," sacerdos Britannicus ad populum suum narravit.

With the end of Roman occupation in Britain, a dark age began on the island. "A dark age is beginning," a British priest told his people.

Post Romanos, Britannia in regna et tribus diversas dividitur. "Regna nostra habemus," rex Britannicus in throno suo dixit.

After the Romans, Britain was divided into different kingdoms and tribes. "We have our kingdoms," a British king said from his throne.

Historia et cultura Romanorum in Britannia diu memorantur. "Romanos meminimus," magister Britannicus in schola docet.

The history and culture of the Romans in Britain were remembered for a long time. "We remember the Romans," a British teacher taught in school.

Exitus Romanorum historiam Britanniae profunde mutat. "Historia nostra mutata est," historiographus Britannicus scripsit.

The departure of the Romans profoundly changed the history of Britain. "Our history has changed," a British historian wrote.

Britannia, post era Romanorum, suam viam in historia invenit. "Viam nostram invenimus," poeta Britannicus in carmine suo cantavit.

After the Roman era, Britain found its own path in history. "We have found our way," a British poet sang in his poem.

Era Romanorum in Britannia, longa et complexa, finem habuit. "Era Romana finita est," civis Britannicus in foro cum amico suo colloquebatur.

The Roman era in Britain, long and complex, came to an end. "The Roman era is over," a British citizen said while conversing with his friend in the forum.

In hoc capitulo, finis aetatis Romanae in Britannia et transitionem ad novam aetatem describitur. Romani, sub oppressionibus et debilitate imperii, Britanniam relinquunt, et tribus Britannicae independentiam et potestatem recuperant. Reliquiae culturae Romanae in insula manent, sed Britannia novam viam in historia sua incipit, a Romanis distinctam. Romanorum in Britannia historia, longa et plena eventuum, finem habet, sed eorum cultura et historia diu in memoria Britannorum manet.

In this chapter, the end of the Roman era in Britain and the transition to a new age are described. The Romans, under pressure and the weakening of the empire, left Britain, and the British tribes regained independence and power. The remnants of Roman culture remained on the island, but Britain began a new path in its history, distinct from the Romans. The Roman history in Britain, long and eventful, came to an end, but their culture and history remained in the memory of the Britons for a long time.

Germania et Roma: Historia Bellorum

Capitulum Primum: Initium Bellorum Germanicorum

*Romani, sub imperio Augusti, Germaniam invadere conati sunt.
"Germaniam invadamus," Augustus in consilio Romae dixit.*

The Romans, under the rule of Augustus, attempted to invade
Germany. "Let us invade Germany," Augustus said in a council at
Rome.

*Germania, terra vasta et silvestris, Romanis incognita erat.
"Terra incognita est," explorator Romanus ad Augustum rettulit.*

Germany, a vast and forested land, was unknown to the Romans.
"It is an unknown land," a Roman scout reported to Augustus.

Romani primas expeditiones in Germaniam fecerunt, terram explorantes. "Explorare debemus," dux Romanus in castris suis dixit.

The Romans made their first expeditions into Germany, exploring the land. "We must explore," a Roman general said in his camp.

Germani, diversis tribus compositi, resistentiam contra Romanos paraverunt. "Romanos resistamus," dux Germanicus in concilio tribuum dixit.

The Germans, composed of various tribes, prepared resistance against the Romans. "Let us resist the Romans," a German leader said in the tribal council.

Publius Quinctilius Varus, dux Romanorum, Germaniam administravit. "Germaniam bene administrabo," Varus ad legiones suas dixit.

Publius Quinctilius Varus, a Roman general, governed Germany. "I will govern Germany well," Varus said to his legions.

Varus legiones Romanas per silvas et campos Germaniae duxit. "Per Germaniam eamus," Varus ad milites suos imperavit.

Varus led the Roman legions through the forests and fields of Germany. "Let us march through Germany," Varus commanded his soldiers.

Arminius, dux Cherusci, contra Romanos consilium secretum cepit. "Insidias Romanis parabimus," Arminius in secreto loco cum sociis suis dixit.

Arminius, leader of the Cherusci, made a secret plan against the Romans. "We will prepare an ambush for the Romans," Arminius said in a secret place to his allies.

Saltus Teutoburgiensis, locus densarum silvarum, locum insidiarum electus est. "Hic insidias ponemus," Arminius ad suos in saltu dixit.

The Teutoburg Forest, a place of dense woods, was chosen as the site of the ambush. "We will set the trap here," Arminius told his men in the forest.

Legiones Romanae in insidias Arminii inciderunt, in saltu Teutoburgiensi. "In insidias incidimus," miles Romanus in saltu clamavit.

The Roman legions fell into Arminius's trap in the Teutoburg Forest. "We've fallen into an ambush," a Roman soldier shouted in the forest.

Clades magna Romanis in Saltu Teutoburgiensi accidit, legiones oppressae sunt. "Clades est," Varus in medio pugnae dixit.

A great disaster befell the Romans in the Teutoburg Forest, and the legions were overwhelmed. "This is a disaster," Varus said in the middle of the battle.

Tres legiones Romanae in pugna deletae sunt, cum multis militibus Romanis cecidisse. "Legiones perditae sunt," nuntius Romanus ad Augustum Romae rettulit.

Three Roman legions were destroyed in the battle, with many Roman soldiers fallen. "The legions are lost," a Roman messenger reported to Augustus in Rome.

Varus, clade accepta, mortem sibi conscivit, desperatione motus. "Mori malo quam captus esse," Varus, mortem sibi consciscens, dixit.

Varus, upon accepting defeat, took his own life in despair. "I prefer to die rather than be captured," Varus said as he took his life.

Augustus, clade Varus nuntiata, magnopere perturbatus est in Roma. "Varus, legiones ubi sunt?" Augustus in palatio suo exclamavit.

When Augustus received the news of Varus's defeat, he was greatly disturbed in Rome. "Varus, where are the legions?" Augustus exclaimed in his palace.

Germani, victoria in Saltu Teutoburgiensi adepti, libertatem suam defenderunt. "Libertatem defendimus," Arminius ad Germanos post victoriam dixit.

The Germans, having achieved victory in the Teutoburg Forest, defended their freedom. "We defend our freedom," Arminius said to the Germans after the victory.

Post cladem Teutoburgiensem, bellum Romanorum in Germania incertum et difficile factum est. "Bellum incertum est," Augustus ad consiliarios suos Romae dixit.

After the defeat at Teutoburg, the Romans' war in Germany became uncertain and difficult. "The war is uncertain," Augustus said to his advisors in Rome.

In hoc capitulo, initium bellorum Germanicorum sub Augusto imperatore describitur. Romani, Germaniam invadere conantes, a Germanis, Arminio duce, in Saltu Teutoburgiensi graviter victi sunt. Clades Teutoburgiensis magnam perturbationem Romanis attulit et incertitudinem bellorum Germanicorum augendam fecit.

In this chapter, the beginning of the Germanic wars under Emperor Augustus is described. The Romans, attempting to invade Germany, were heavily defeated by the Germans, led by Arminius, in the Teutoburg Forest. The disaster of Teutoburg brought great disturbance to the Romans and increased the uncertainty of the Germanic wars.

Capitulum Secundum: Germanicus et Expeditio Ultionis

Germanicus, Caesaris nepos, expeditionem ultionis in Germaniam paravit. "Ultionem capiamus," Germanicus ad consilium Romanum dixit.

Germanicus, nephew of Caesar, prepared a campaign of revenge into Germany. "Let us take revenge," Germanicus said to the Roman council.

Copias Romanas in Germaniam duxit, propositum vindictae habens. "In Germaniam eamus," Germanicus ad legiones suas imperavit.

He led Roman troops into Germany, with the goal of vengeance. "Let us go into Germany," Germanicus ordered his legions.

Reliquias cladi Teutoburgiensis visitavit, casus militum Romanorum recordans. "Reliquias visitare debemus," Germanicus in loco cladi dixit.

He visited the remains of the Teutoburg disaster, remembering the fallen Roman soldiers. "We must visit the remains," Germanicus said at the site of the disaster.

Multas pugnas contra Germanos gessit, terram hostium penetrans. "Pugnemus," Germanicus ad milites suos in acie dixit.

He fought many battles against the Germans, penetrating the enemy's land. "Let us fight," Germanicus said to his soldiers on the battlefield.

Arminius, dux Germanorum, Germanicum et Romanos fortiter oppugnavit. "Romanos repellamus," Arminius ad suos Germanos clamavit.

Arminius, leader of the Germans, fiercely attacked Germanicus and the Romans. "Let us repel the Romans," Arminius shouted to his fellow Germans.

Pugnae asperae in silvis et paludibus Germaniae fiebant. "Silvis nos protegimus," dux Germanicus in silva dixit.

Harsh battles took place in the forests and marshes of Germany. "We are protected by the forests," a German leader said in the woods.

Germanicus in Germania quasdam victorias reportavit, hostes superans. "Victoriam habemus," Germanicus post proelium nuntiavit.

Germanicus won some victories in Germany, defeating the enemy. "We have victory," Germanicus announced after the battle.

Legiones Romanae manuballistas et catapultas in pugnis adhibuerunt. "Arma iaciamus," ballistarius Romanus in acie clamavit.

The Roman legions used ballistae and catapults in the battles. "Let us fire the weapons," a Roman artilleryman shouted on the battlefield.

Germani, calliditate usi, Romanos saepe in insidiis ceperunt. "Insidias Romanis struamus," Arminius ad suos dixit.

The Germans, using cunning, often caught the Romans in ambushes. "Let us set traps for the Romans," Arminius said to his men.

Germanicum, Arminium captare conantem, successu caruit. "Arminium capere non possumus," Germanicus ad legatum suum dixit.

Germanicus, attempting to capture Arminius, failed in his efforts. "We cannot capture Arminius," Germanicus said to his lieutenant.

Tiberius, Romanorum imperator, Germanicum a pugna in Germania revocavit. "Germanicum revocemus," Tiberius in Roma decrevit.

Tiberius, the emperor of the Romans, recalled Germanicus from the fight in Germany. "Let us recall Germanicus," Tiberius decreed in Rome.

Romam reversus, Germanicus triumphum magnificum egit. "Triumphum agamus," Germanicus in Romam ingressus exclamavit.

Returning to Rome, Germanicus held a magnificent triumph. "Let us celebrate the triumph," Germanicus exclaimed as he entered Rome.

Inter Germanos, Arminius ut liberator et heros celebratus est. "Arminius liberator noster est," Germanus in concilio dixit.

Among the Germans, Arminius was celebrated as a liberator and hero. "Arminius is our liberator," a German said in a council.

Post expeditionem, Germanicus in Orientem ad alia bella missus est. "In Orientem ire debeo," Germanicus in Roma cogitavit.

After the campaign, Germanicus was sent to the East for other wars. "I must go to the East," Germanicus thought in Rome.

Bellum Romanorum in Germania sine decisiva victoria finitum est. "Bellum finem habet," legatus Romanus ad senatum Romam rettulit.

The Roman war in Germany ended without a decisive victory. "The war is over," a Roman envoy reported to the Senate in Rome.

In hoc capitulo, narratur de expeditione ultionis Germanici, Caesaris nepotis, contra Germanos post cladem Teutoburgiensem. Germanicus in Germaniam copias Romanas duxit, multas pugnas gessit, sed Arminium, ducem Germanorum, capere non potuit. Post varia proelia et sine certa victoria, Germanicus a Tiberio imperatore revocatus est et Romam reversus triumphum egit. Arminius inter Germanos ut liberator celebratus est, et bellum in Germania sine clara victoria Romanorum finitum est.

In this chapter, the revenge campaign of Germanicus, the nephew of Caesar, against the Germans after the Teutoburg disaster is described. Germanicus led Roman troops into Germany, fought many battles, but could not capture Arminius, the leader of the Germans. After various battles and without a clear victory, Germanicus was recalled by Emperor Tiberius and returned to Rome, where he celebrated a triumph. Arminius was celebrated as a liberator among the Germans, and the war in Germany ended without a clear Roman victory.

Capitulum Tertium: Limes Germanicus

Romani, Germaniam plene subigere non valentes, limitem, murum et fossam, construxerunt. "Limitem construamus," architectus Romanus ad imperatorem dixit.

The Romans, unable to fully conquer Germany, built the limes, a wall and ditch. "Let us build the limes," a Roman architect said to the emperor.

Limes, structura immanis, Romanorum fines contra Germanos protegebat. "Fines nostros custodiamus," praefectus Romanus ad milites suos in limite dixit.

The limes, a massive structure, protected the Roman borders against the Germans. "Let us guard our borders," a Roman prefect said to his soldiers at the limes.

Castella et turres per limitem aedificata sunt, custodiam firmantes. "Castella et turres aedificemus," ingenarius Romanus in limite laborans dixit.

Forts and towers were built along the limes, strengthening the defense. "Let us build forts and towers," a Roman engineer working on the limes said.

Milites Romani in limite steterunt, finium custodes. "In limite stetimus," miles Romanus ad commilitonem suum in castello dixit.

Roman soldiers stood at the limes, guarding the borders. "We stood at the limes," a Roman soldier said to his comrade in the fort.

Commercia inter Romanos et Germanos per limitem frequentia fiebant. "Commercia cum Germanis habeamus," negotiator Romanus in limite dixit.

Trade between the Romans and the Germans frequently occurred across the limes. "Let us trade with the Germans," a Roman merchant said at the limes.

Cultura Romana paulatim ad Germanos transibat, utentibus Romanis. "Cultura nostra transgreditur," magister Romanus ad discipulum Germanum dixit.

Roman culture gradually passed to the Germans through Roman influence. "Our culture is spreading," a Roman teacher said to a German student.

Germani, Romanorum militum consuetudines et artes discebant. "Discamus ab Romanis," iuvenis Germanus ad patrem suum dixit.

The Germans learned the customs and skills of the Roman soldiers. "Let us learn from the Romans," a young German said to his father.

Limes, saepe incursionibus Germanorum fortiter resistebat. "Resistamus," centurio Romanus ad milites in limite clamavit.

The limes often strongly resisted German incursions. "Let us resist," a Roman centurion shouted to his soldiers at the limes.

Paces interdum inter Romanos et Germanos stabilitae erant. "Pacem faciamus," legatus Romanus ad ducem Germanum in colloquio dixit.

Peace was sometimes established between the Romans and the Germans. "Let us make peace," a Roman envoy said to the German leader in a meeting.

Germani interdum conducticios Romanis praebebant, ad auxilium. "Auxiliarii simus," dux Germanicus ad suos dixit.

The Germans sometimes provided mercenaries to the Romans for assistance. "Let us be auxiliaries," a German leader said to his men.

Limes Romanorum in Germania longum tempus stetit, monumentum magni momenti. "Limes manebit," senex Romanus ad iuvenem in limite dixit.

The Roman limes in Germany stood for a long time, a monument of great importance. "The limes will remain," an old Roman said to a young man at the limes.

Germani, libertatem suam servantes, limitem Romanorum respectabant. "Libertatem nostram servemus," Germanus in villa sua dixit.

The Germans, preserving their freedom, respected the Roman limes. "Let us preserve our freedom," a German said in his villa.

Limes, civilisationis Romanae terminus, in historia Romana magni momenti erat. "Limes finis noster est," historiographus Romanus in libro suo scripsit.

The limes, the boundary of Roman civilization, was of great importance in Roman history. "The limes is our boundary," a Roman historian wrote in his book.

Germania, per limitem, et Roma et barbaros coniungens, culturas. "Duae culturae coniunguntur," philosophus Romanus in limite meditabatur.

Through the limes, Germany connected both Rome and the barbarians, merging cultures. "Two cultures are coming together," a Roman philosopher meditated at the limes.

Limes, historiae Romanae pars, in monumentis et annalibus manet, testimonium temporis. "Limes in historia nostra manebit," scriptor Romanus in annalibus dixit.

The limes, part of Roman history, remains in monuments and records, a witness of the times. "The limes will remain in our history," a Roman writer said in the annals.

In hoc capitulo, descriptio limitis Germanici, murus et fossa quae Romanorum fines in Germania protegebat, enarratur. Limes castellis et turribus munitus erat, milites Romanos custodientes. Commercia et cultura inter Romanos et Germanos per limitem fiebant. Limes incursionibus Germanorum resistebat, et paces interdum stabilitae erant. Limes longum tempus stetit, et in monumentis et historia Romana manet, civilisationis Romanae terminus et monumentum historiarum Romanorum et Germanorum.

In this chapter, the description of the Germanic limes, the wall and ditch that protected Roman borders in Germany, is narrated. The limes was fortified with forts and towers, guarding Roman soldiers. Trade and culture flowed between the Romans and Germans across the limes. The limes resisted German incursions, and peace was sometimes established. The limes stood for a long time, and it remains in monuments and Roman history, a boundary of Roman civilization and a monument to the histories of both the Romans and Germans.

Capitulum Quartum: Conflictus Continuus

Bellum inter Romanos et Germanos saepe renovabatur, conflictus sine fine. "Iterum bellum geramus," imperator Romanus in palatio suo dixit.

The war between the Romans and the Germans was often renewed, a conflict without end. "Let us wage war again," the Roman emperor said in his palace.

Dux Romanus, periculis Germanorum semper conscius, vigilans manebat. "Vigilare debemus," dux ad milites suos in castris clamavit.

The Roman general, always aware of the dangers from the Germans, remained vigilant. "We must stay alert," the general shouted to his soldiers in the camp.

Germani, Romanorum incursionibus fortiter resistebant. "Romanos repellemus," dux Germanicus ad suos in silva dixit.

The Germans strongly resisted the incursions of the Romans. "We will repel the Romans," the German leader said to his men in the forest.

Excursiones et incursiones per limitem Germanicum fieri solebant. "Per limitem moveamur," explorator Romanus ad ducem suum in limite proposuit.

Excursions and incursions often took place along the Germanic limes. "Let us move along the limes," the Roman scout proposed to his commander at the limes.

Imperatores Romani Germaniam saepe petebant, terram vastam et rebellem. "Germaniam iterum petamus," imperator Romanus ad senatum dixit.

The Roman emperors often targeted Germany, a vast and rebellious land. "Let us once again seek Germany," the Roman emperor said to the senate.

Germani, ducibus audacibus ducti, Romanos fortiter oppugnabant. "Pro libertate nostra pugnemus," dux Germanicus in acie clamavit.

The Germans, led by bold leaders, fiercely attacked the Romans. "Let us fight for our freedom," the German leader shouted on the battlefield.

Natura Germaniae, Romano militi, multas difficultates praebuit. "Terra haec difficilis est," miles Romanus in palude Germaniae dixit.

The nature of Germany presented many difficulties to the Roman soldier. "This land is difficult," a Roman soldier said in the marshes of Germany.

Germani, silvis et paludibus utentes, Romanos saepe eludebant. "Silvis nos protegamus," Germanus in consilio cum sociis suis dixit.

The Germans, using the forests and marshes, often eluded the Romans. "Let us protect ourselves with the forests," a German said in council with his comrades.

Romanorum fortitudo a Germanis saepe probata est, in proeliis asperis. "Fortes esse debemus," centurio Romanus ad milites suos in acie hortabatur.

The strength of the Romans was often tested by the Germans in harsh battles. "We must be strong," the Roman centurion encouraged his soldiers on the battlefield.

Pugnae et proelia inter Romanos et Germanos erant aspera et cruenta. "Proelia dura sunt," miles Romanus ad commilitonem suum post pugnam dixit.

The fights and battles between the Romans and the Germans were rough and bloody. "The battles are hard," a Roman soldier said to his comrade after the fight.

Imperatores Romani Germanos subigere conabantur, sed frustra. "Germanos subigamus," imperator Romanus in strategico consilio dixit.

The Roman emperors tried to subjugate the Germans, but in vain. "Let us subdue the Germans," the Roman emperor said in a strategic council.

Germani, libertate cari, Romanos constanter repudiabant. "Libertatem nostram servemus," dux Germanicus ad populum suum in concilio dixit.

The Germans, dear to their freedom, constantly rejected the Romans. "Let us preserve our freedom," the German leader said to his people in council.

Bellum inter Romanos et Germanos longum et arduum erat, sine victoria clara. "Bellum longum est," historiographus Romanus in annalibus scripsit.

The war between the Romans and the Germans was long and arduous, without a clear victory. "The war is long," a Roman historian wrote in the annals.

Germani, culturae suae fidi, Romanis fortiter resistebant. "Culturae nostrae fideles simus," sacerdos Germanicus ad tribum suam dixit.

The Germans, faithful to their culture, strongly resisted the Romans. "Let us be faithful to our culture," a German priest said to his tribe.

Romanorum in Germania bellum historiam belli ipsius mutavit, complexum et indeterminatum. "Historia nostra mutatur," philosophus Romanus in Roma meditabatur.

The war of the Romans in Germany changed the history of the war itself, making it complex and indeterminate. "Our history is changing," a Roman philosopher meditated in Rome.

In hoc capitulo, conflictus continuus inter Romanos et Germanos describitur. Bellum inter duas potentias, cum incursionibus, excursionibus, et proeliis asperis, diuturnum et arduum erat. Imperatores Romani Germaniam subigere frustra conabantur, et Germani, libertate sua cari, Romanos constanter repudiabant. Hoc bellum historiam Romanorum et Germanorum profundum et indeterminatum effectum habuit.

In this chapter, the continuous conflict between the Romans and Germans is described. The war between the two powers, with incursions, excursions, and harsh battles, was long and arduous. The Roman emperors tried in vain to subjugate Germany, and the Germans, dear to their freedom, constantly rejected the Romans. This war profoundly and indeterminately affected the history of both the Romans and Germans.

Capitulum Quintum: Finis Bellorum et Legatum

Germanicis bellis finis paulatim advenit, aetas conflictuum finiens. "Bellum finem habet," dux Romanus in consilio dixit.

The end of the Germanic wars slowly approached, bringing an era of conflicts to a close. "The war has an end," the Roman general said in council.

Romani, Germaniam plene non vincendo, pacem cum Germanis faciunt. "Pacem faciamus," legatus Romanus ad Germanos proposuit.

The Romans, not fully conquering Germany, made peace with the Germans. "Let us make peace," the Roman envoy proposed to the Germans.

Germani, a Romanis non subacti, libertatem suam servaverunt. "Libertatem nostram servavimus," dux Germanicus in concilio populi sui dixit.

The Germans, not subdued by the Romans, preserved their freedom. "We have preserved our freedom," the German leader said to his people in council.

Cultura et commercium inter Romanos et Germanos sensim crescunt. "Commercium nobiscum augeatur," mercator Romanus ad Germanum dixit.

Culture and trade between the Romans and Germans gradually grew. "Let trade between us grow," a Roman merchant said to a German.

Germania, fine bellorum, in historia sua novam paginam vertit. "Nova aetas incipit," historiographus Germanus in annalibus suis scripsit.

Germany, with the end of the wars, turned a new page in its history. "A new era begins," a German historian wrote in his annals.

Romani, Germanorum terras non capientes, fines Imperii custodiunt. "Fines nostros custodiamus," praefectus Romanus in limite dixit.

The Romans, not capturing the lands of the Germans, guarded the borders of the Empire. "Let us guard our borders," a Roman prefect said at the limes.

Germani, cultura Romana affecti, novam aetatem et viam incipiunt. "Novas vias ambulemus," iuvenis Germanus in vico suo dixit.

The Germans, influenced by Roman culture, began a new age and path. "Let us walk new paths," a young German said in his village.

Relationes inter Romanos et Germanos, bellis finitis, meliorantur. "Amicitiam colamus," legatus Romanus ad Germanum dixit.

Relations between the Romans and Germans, with the wars ended, improved. "Let us cultivate friendship," the Roman envoy said to the German.

Germani, in historia Romana, magnam partem habent. "Partem nostram in historia agnoscimus," dux Germanicus ad suos dixit.

The Germans played a major role in Roman history. "We recognize our part in history," the German leader said to his people.

Romani, bellorum finem agnoscentes, ad alia in Imperio se vertunt. "Alia agenda sunt," imperator Romanus in Roma dixit.

The Romans, acknowledging the end of the wars, turned to other matters in the Empire. "Other matters must be attended to," the Roman emperor said in Rome.

Pax inter Romanos et Germanos multa beneficia utrique populo attulit. "Pax nobis beneficia affert," senator Romanus in senatu dixit.

The peace between the Romans and Germans brought many benefits to both peoples. "Peace brings us benefits," a Roman senator said in the senate.

Legatum bellorum, in monumentis et historiis, manet testimonium temporum. "Historiam scribamus," scriptor Romanus in bibliotheca sua dixit.

The legacy of the wars, in monuments and histories, remains as a testament of the times. "Let us write the history," a Roman writer said in his library.

Narratio bellorum inter Romanos et Germanos historiam Europae profundum effecit. "Historiam Europae formavimus," philosophus Romanus meditabatur.

The story of the wars between the Romans and Germans profoundly shaped European history. "We have shaped the history of Europe," a Roman philosopher meditated.

Germania, a Romanis intacta, viam suam unicam in historia invenit. "Viam nostram invenimus," poeta Germanus in carmine suo cantavit.

Germany, untouched by the Romans, found its own unique path in history. "We have found our own way," a German poet sang in his poem.

Bellorum finis, aetatem novam in Germania et Roma inchoavit, mundum mutans. "Nova aetas inchoatur," civis Romanus in foro cum amico suo colloquebatur.

The end of the wars began a new era in Germany and Rome, changing the world. "A new era begins," a Roman citizen said, conversing with a friend in the forum.

In hoc capitulo, finis bellorum Germanicorum et legatum eorum in historia Romana et Germanica narratur. Pax inter Romanos et Germanos beneficia utrique populo attulit, et relationes inter eos

In this chapter, the end of the Germanic wars and their legacy in Roman and German history is narrated. The peace between the Romans and Germans brought benefits to both peoples, and relations between them improved. The Germans, preserving their freedom, and the Romans, turning to other matters in the Empire, opened a new page in their history. The story of the wars, remaining in annals and monuments, profoundly shaped the history of Europe.

More books

More ressources

Endorsements by leading Latinists

All on **discoverlatin.com**